The Grand Ol Duke of York

A Pantomime

Norman Robbins

Samuel French – London
New York – Sydney – Toronto – Hollywood

For Mum and Dad
who gave me the idea

AUTHOR'S NOTE

Like my previous pantomimes, *The Grand Old Duke of York* is written for easy staging, but can, of course, be performed as lavishly as required. I have alternated full or half sets with lane scenes throughout, and kept sound effects, props and lighting as simple as possible.

The Guardian of the Cave I leave to the imagination and ingenuity of the director, purely for reasons of space and availability. From my own experiences in staging amateur pantomimes, I know that great difficulty is often encountered when trying to obtain Giants, Dragons, Sea serpents, etc., for particular productions, as some other local group has always managed to collar the only one available for miles—and for exactly the same period of time that you needed it. Therefore, for *this* pantomime, simply find out what *is* available and use that. Anything from a giant to a skeleton will work.

Characters should create no difficulty. All are traditional types and easily recognized.

Music should be bright and cheerful, and in my original conception of the show, I drew heavily on Musical Comedy items.

Keep the pace brisk and above all, enjoy yourselves.

Factual details

The character of Mother Shipton actually existed. Born Ursula Sonthiel, in Knaresborough, Yorkshire, 1488, her mis-shaped body and coarse features soon earned her the reputation of being a witch. Her startling prophesies brought her great fame, and amongst the many events she foretold (reputedly) were the launching of iron ships, manned flight, the discovery of radio, motor cars and World Wars I and II. She died on the day she foretold at the appointed time. Her famous dropping-well is known the world over for its petrifying properties, and visitors to her cave may see stone knitting and hats, etc., plus a collection of items still in the process of being transformed.

Frederick of York is another factual character, though it is doubted that he ever commanded ten thousand men. He was, however, very popular with his troops and an accomplished commander-in-chief. My interpretation of his character is purely for the purpose of this pantomime and is not intended to be a true one. The famous hill upon which he allegedly marched his troops has resisted all attempts to locate it. Certainly none in the York area fit the bill. This being the case, my explanation of its whereabouts is, I suppose, as good as anyone else's.

Norman Robbins 1980

CHARACTERS

Baron Snatcher of Seizitt Hall

Martha Muffett, ex-nurserymaid to the Duke

Jack
Jill } the City watercarriers

Colin, a Gypsy boy

Old Mother Shipton, the famous witch of Knaresborough

Tommy Tucker, Martha's beau

Pye
Peas } the Baron's henchmen

Melody, the Grand Duke's ward

The Grand Old Duke of York, a warrior (or worrier)

Maleficent, a bad-tempered fairy

The Guardian of the Cave

Chorus of **Soldiers, Citizens, Servants, Guards, Courtiers, Gypsies,** etc.

Babes and Junior chorus of **Denizens of the Wood, Toy Soldiers, Pixies, Hobgoblins,** etc.

ACT I

Scene 1   The Ancient City of York
Scene 2   A Path in Acomb Woods
Scene 3   Inside the Mansion House of the Grand Old
       Duke
Scene 4   Down Whip-ma Whop-ma Lane
Scene 5   The City Square

ACT II

Scene 1   Half-way up the Enchanted Hill
Scene 2   A Rocky Gorge
Scene 3   Inside the Enchanted Hill
Scene 4   A Quiet Path on the Hillside
Scene 5   The Throneroom of the Black Castle
Scene 6   The Dungeons of the Black Castle
Scene 7   The City Square
Scene 8   A Corridor in the Grand Duke's Mansion
       House
Scene 9   The Mansion House and Finale

ACT I

Scene 1

The Ancient City of York

A pantomime adaptation of the City Square, with half-timbered cottages standing before a backdrop of low, wooded hills. Martha Muffett's cottage is UR *and other houses and shops etc., are* L

When the CURTAIN *rises, it is the day of the Annual Fayre, and the Citizens of York are enjoying themselves as they sing and dance. Peddlars, puppeteers, sweetmeat-vendors, balloon-sellers, etc., mingle with them. The setting is as bright and cheerful as possible*

SONG 1

At the end of the song, all chatter merrily

> *Baron Snatcher enters* UL, *and the merriment dies away. He is dressed all in black, has a grim scowl on his face and carries a whip. Elbowing his way through the throng he moves* C

Boy (*calling*) Look out, everybody. It's Baron Snatcher of Seizitt Hall!

The Citizens boo

Baron (*snarling*) Silence, you scurvy dogs. (*He glares at them till they subside*) I want all this rubbish cleared away and the streets emptied before I count five. Understand?

Girl (*stepping forward*) *Rubbish? What* rubbish, Baron Snatcher? This— (*indicating*)—is the Annual Fayre.

Baron (*sneering*) Bah! It's just an excuse for you idle, good-for-nothing lot to sneak another day off work.

Boy (*indignantly*) No it isn't. We've always been allowed a day off work to come to the Fayre—(*to the others*)—haven't we?

The others agree

Baron (*with an evil smile*) Oh, you have, have you? Well I've got *news* for you. Some very *good* news.

Boy (*eagerly*) Leaving York, are you?

Baron (*annoyed*) No, I am *not*. (*More calmly*) As a matter of fact, I've just managed to get myself elected High Sheriff of York.

They all react in surprise

> And my first new law is to *cancel the Fayre*. Now and forever. (*He smirks*)

Girl You can't do *that*.

They all agree

Baron (*cracking his whip*) Who says I can't? (*He glares at them*) Now I'm High Sheriff I can do just what I want, so clear off or I'll have you all thrown into the City gaol. (*He leers*)

The Crowd boo and hiss as he menaces them, but gather up their things and exit with much grumbling and black looks

(*To the audience*) That'll teach 'em to have respect for their betters. (*He smirks*) There's going to be quite a few changes around here now that *I'm* in charge. (*He indicates Martha's cottage*) You see that cottage there? It belongs to an interfering, loud-mouthed, nosey old faggot called Martha Muffet. According to my records, she hasn't paid a penny rent in over ten years . . . So today—seeing as how it's her birthday— I'm going to throw her into the street. (*He laughs and crosses over to the cottage to hammer on the door*) Come out, you flea-bitten old gasbag!

Martha Muffet enters DR

Martha (*chatting to the audience*) Hello, dears. How are you? All right? Enjoying yourself, love? That's the spirit. That's what we're all here for isn't it? Nothing like a good laugh. (*She catches sight of the Baron*) Hello—looks like someone's left the manhole cover off the sewer again.

Baron (*turning*) Ahaaaaaaa! Just the woman I want. (*He marches up to her*)

Martha (*patting her hair*) Too late. I'm already spoken for.

Baron I want my rent money.

Martha (*giving a sigh of relief*) Thank goodness for that. I thought you wanted mine.

Baron (*snarling*) I mean yours, you addle-pated old twerp. Hand it over at once. (*He holds out his hand*)

Martha Here—watch it, fishface. You're talking to a lady now—not your mother.

Baron (*sneering*) Lady? Hah. You wouldn't know what a lady was if she ran you over with a steamroller.

Martha Oh, no? Well, let me tell *you*, *I* once followed the Grand Duke's procession down Gillygate when he rode in his horse-drawn carriage.

Baron Yes, with a bucket and shovel in your hands. Now do I get what's coming to me, or don't I?

Martha Oh—if only you *could*.

Baron Right. Then that's done it. As new High Sheriff of York, I intend to make a clean sweep of the City—and I'm starting with *you*.

Martha Oh. Would you like to borrow my sweeping-brush to do it with? I'll go get it for you.

She dashes into her cottage

Baron What? (*He realizes*) Of course I don't want to borrow your sweeping-brush, you idiotic old hasbeen. Come back here at once. Did you hear me? Come back. This instant.

Martha dashes out again with a broom, sweeping furiously and showering him with dust

(*anguished*) Aghhhhhhhh! I'm covered in dust.

Martha (*pausing to peer at him*) So you are. Here—you didn't ought to be running round looking like that, you know. Folks'll think you can't afford to have it cleaned.

Baron (*livid*) Wipe it off at once!

Martha quickly scrubs him down with the broom

Aghhhhhhhhh! Now it's ten times worse. (*He snatches the broom from her and tosses it aside in a fury*)

Martha Temper, temper. (*To the audience*) Oooh, some folks are never satisfied.

Baron (*with great malevolence*) Just you *wait*. By the time I've finished with you, you'll wish you'd never been *born*. In five minutes' time, I'll have my henchmen here to toss you into the street.

Martha (*startled*) Eh? Here—you can't do that. I owe you more rent money than anybody else in York. I deserve some consideration, I do.

Baron (*snarling*) You'll get no consideration from *me*, you old crackpot.

Martha But—but—but ... If you throw me out—I'll have nowhere to live. And besides—you'll never get your rent money.

Baron So what? I've decided at long last to *cut my losses* and do myself a favour.

Martha In that case, why not cut your *throat* and do *everybody* one?

Baron Bah.

He exits L in a very bad temper

Martha (*to the audience*) That's torn it, boys and girls. I'm going to be turned out of my little cottage. Whatever am I going to do? (*Her face crumples*)

Jack and Jill enter. They are about sixteen and the City's watercarriers. Jack holds a long envelope in his hand

Jack
Jill } (*moving towards her*) Hello, Martha. { (*Together*)

Martha (*sniffling*) Hello, Jack and Jill. (*She begins to sob*)

Jack (*putting his arm around her*) Come on, Martha. Cheer up. Don't let *that* old villain upset you.

Jill *We* heard *everything*. (*She laughs*) Honestly, if you'd said just one more word, I think he'd have exploded on the spot.

Martha (*disgustedly*) Trust *me* to shut my big mouth at the wrong time.

(*She dabs at her eyes*)

Jack (*bitterly*) I wish someone would put him in his place.

Jill Here, here.

Martha I'd do it meself—if I could afford to buy the shovel to dig it with. (*She sniffles*) But here I am. Penniless. And he's going to turn me out of my little cottage. (*She begins to sob again*)

Jack He wouldn't dare.

Jill Of course he wouldn't. Just because he's the new High Sheriff, it doesn't mean he's got all the power in York. If the Grand Old Duke ever realized what was going on behind his back, he'd soon put his foot down.

Martha Yes, and knowing Baron Snatcher, *he'd* most probably *stamp* on it. (*She sniffles*) You know—I've lived in that place all me life—nearly twenty-eight years. When I moved in there it was only a Wendy house. (*Pensively*) Mind you, I've not been able to use the back bedroom for some time. Not since they built that nudist camp in the field down the road.

Jack Oh?

Martha Well, you see, I might see something that would embarrass me if I happened to glance out of the window by accident.

Jill I don't think *that's* very likely, Martha. There's a very tall fence running all the way round it, not to mention the high trees. You wouldn't be able to see anything at all, I'm sure.

Martha I can if I stand on top of the wardrobe with my binoculars. (*She sighs deeply*) Oh, well. I suppose I'd better go in and start packing. (*She turns to exit*)

Jack Wait. Surely there must be someone who could lend you some rent money? What about Tommy?

Jill Yes. He was telling us only the other day that he came from a very rich family.

Martha Tommy Tucker? A rich family? He's got to be joking. His family were so poor his little *sister* had to be made in Japan. And anyway, I couldn't ask *him*. We're not even on speaking terms at the moment.

Jill Why's that?

Martha Well, the last time we went out together, I ended up having to smack his face for him.

Jack Whatever for?

Martha I wanted to check he was still *alive*.

Jill (*laughing*) Poor Tommy. He's not the most romantic of men, is he?

Martha You're telling me. The only time I get a good squeeze lately, is when I wear my tight corsets. Still, I'm not worried. I've got other fish to fry. (*She glances round to make sure she is not overheard*) Last week, I sent off one of my photographs to a Lonely Heart's Club.

Jack A Lonely Heart's Club?

Martha Yes. And I'm expecterating a reply any time now. (*She beams*)

Jack Oh—well perhaps *this* is it. (*He holds up the letter*) We were just on our way to deliver it to you.

Martha (*excited*) Ooooh, let me look. (*She takes it*) It is. (*Reading*) "To Martha Muffet from the Lonely Heart's Club."

Jill (*all agog*) What does it say?

Martha (*opening the letter and reading*) "Dear Martha, we're not *that* lonely." (*Her face crumples*)

Jack (*comforting her*) Oh, never mind, Martha. There are plenty more fish in the sea.

Martha Yes—but who wants to marry a halibut? (*She sobs*) Ohhh. E-jected and re-jected all in one day. I may as well go throw myself into the river and have done with it.

Jill Don't cry, Martha. Nothing is ever as bad as it seems.

Martha Have you watched (*well-known TV series*) lately? (*She sniffles*) No? I know when I'm not wanted. I'll go pack me things and leave.

Jill No. Wait. Why not tell the Grand Old Duke that you're being turned out? He'll never stand by and see you homeless. After all, didn't you once work for him?

Martha (*shocked*) Oh, I couldn't go to *him*. Not after what happened. No, I'll just have to go. (*She breaks down*) It was all my fault, anyway.

She scurries off into her cottage sobbing

Jill (*puzzled*) Did I say something I shouldn't have said, Jack?

Jack I'm afraid you did. You see, long before we were born, Martha was nursemaid to the Grand Old Duke's baby, and as she was always so very busy, she used to hang the child's cradle on top of an old apple tree that grew outside the nursery window. When the wind blew, you see, the cradle would rock the baby to sleep. But one terrible day, a sudden gust of wind snapped off the branch that held the cradle, and down it went. Cradle, baby and all.

Jill How awful. And was the baby hurt?

Jack No-one knows, because when they rushed out into the street, all they found was the cradle and the broken branch. The baby had vanished completely. Of course, poor Martha blamed herself, even though the Grand Old Duke insisted that she couldn't possibly be held responsible. She left the Mansion House in tears and so far as I know, has never been back since.

Jill What a sad story. No wonder she was so upset at what I said. (*She pauses to think*) Still—if she won't go and see the Grand Old Duke herself, there's nothing to stop *us* from doing it for her, is there?

Jack You're right. We'll go and see him at once. (*He turns to exit*)

Jill (*holding back*) If only we could think up some way to get Tommy to set a wedding date, too. I'm sure *that* would help matters.

Jack (*chidingly*) Now you leave Tommy alone. He can decide for himself if he's ready for marrying.

Jill But Jack, I'm sure that all she *really* needs is a nice young man to look after her.

Jack (*smiling*) Isn't that what all the ladies need?

Jill Certainly not. *I* can look after myself.

Jack Can you?

SONG 2

At the end of the song, they exit DR *holding hands. As they do so, Colin enters* L. *He is dressed in ragged Gypsy costume and carries a stick over his shoulder with a red-cloth bag tied to it. He moves* DC *glancing about him as he does*

Colin So this is York. Thank goodness I've arrived at last. Now perhaps I can find some work at the Fayre and begin to eat again. (*He looks round again*) But where is it? There's no-one around. I thought York Fayre was supposed to be a large one. (*Brightly*) I know, I'll ask at this house. (*He crosses to a house* L, *and raps at the door*)

1st Voice (*off*) Clear off! We want no Gypsies here.

Colin (*shrugging*) Hmmm. I'd better try another one. (*He moves to another house and knocks*)

2nd Voice (*off*) Be off with you, or I'll set the dogs at your heels!

Colin (*taking a step back*) It seems that I'm not welcome here. Perhaps I'd better forget about finding work and move on to Harrogate.

He begins to exit DL. *As he does so, Mother Shipton Enters* UR. *She is dressed like a Welsh witch and carries a wooden spoon which is used like a wand*

Mother Shipton (*cheerily*) One moment, Colin. Hark to me.
'Tis here you'll find your destiny.

Colin turns in surprise to face her

When trouble comes—as soon it will
To those who march on yonder hill—
(*she indicates off* L *with her spoon*)—
It's you alone who'll save the day
If you take note of all I say.

Colin Me? But how? I mean—what makes you so sure?
And who are you?

Mother Shipton My boy, there's naught in this world I
Cannot divine or prophesy.
I've given Knaresboro' town its fame . . .
Old Mother Shipton is my name. (*She gives him a curtsy*)

Colin (*stepping back*) A witch. (*He moves slowly away from her*)

Mother Shipton (*laughing*) Aye. A witch. But one that's *good*,
I'd like that *clearly* understood.
Here today to aid your cause,
So listen, now. Your footsteps pause.

Colin halts cautiously and she indicates with her spoon the surroundings

Within these ancient City walls
The voice of Strange Adventure calls.
So trust in me and magic's laws
And I promise quite soon that York will be yours.

With a light laugh, she swirls around and exits R

Colin (*calling*) Wait. (*He runs* UR, *as if to follow her*) Wait. (*He halts*) She's gone. (*He moves back* DC *in a daze*) Was I dreaming? Did I really see the famous witch, Old Mother Shipton? And if so, what could she have meant? How can a poor Gypsy boy like me own a great City like York? It's impossible. (*He thinks*) And yet—Dick Whittington was only a poor boy and *he* became Lord Mayor of *London*. (*Brightening*) Well, perhaps I'd better stay here after all. Then if fame and fortune *do* come looking for me, I'm going to be right here waiting for them.

SONG 3

After the song, he exits happily DL. *As soon as he has gone, Tommy Tucker dashes in* UR *hastily buttoning his shirt and tucking the tail into his trousers. He moves* C

Tommy (*looking into the audience*) Ooooh, ecky thump. They've not started already, have they? (*He looks at his watch*) That's torn it. I was supposed to be here at the beginning. (*He looks into the wings*) They—er—they've not been asking for me, have they? You know—that lot behind there, the stage manager and the producer. Tucker's the name. *Tommy* Tucker. (*As the audience respond*) You're sure? You're not having me on? (*He sighs with relief*) Thank goodness for that. You know every time I get here late they make me do all the washing-up at the interval. They do. Honest. I've been in so much hot water lately, my hands look like lumps of tripe. But I'll tell you why I'm late. It's because I've just been to the doctor's. Ooooh, I hate going to the doctor, don't you? Aren't them stethoscopes cold? If I hadn't been feeling so poorly I wouldn't have gone at all. I had to take all me clothes off. Even me cap. He took one look at me, did the doctor—one look—and he went as white as a sheet. "What is it?" I said. "What's wrong with me?" "I don't know", he replied. "But if you were a building, I'd have to have you condemned." And then he gave me an injection. Penicillin. Oooh, ever such a lot of it he put in his little needle. Well, I'll give you an idea of how much there was. Every time I breath out, I cure ten other people. Mind you, it doesn't half make you tired, that penicillin. I'm so tired I can hardly keep my eyes open. In fact—if I'm not careful, I won't stay awake long enough to sing for me supper. And you know what happens if you get tired, don't you? You forget things. I even forget my *own name*. I do. So I'll tell you what, just to help me remember it, every time I come on and shout: "Hiya, kids" will you shout back: "Hiya, Tommy"? Will you? Right. Let's have a little practice. (*He shouts*) Hiya, kids. (*Audience reaction*) Ooooooooooooh. That was *rotten*. You'll have to do better than that. Come on. Let's try it again. All the fellers loosen your ties and undo your top buttons, and all the women—well, you'd better make your own arrangements. Altogether now. (*He calls*) Hiya, kids. (*Reaction*) That was smashing. Now don't forget. As soon as I . . .

Colin enters DL

Hello. I've not seen this feller round here before. I'd better just
introduce myself to him. (*To Colin*) Hello. I'm Tommy Tucker.

Colin (*smiling*) Hello. I'm Colin.

Tommy Are you a stranger round here?

Colin That's right. I've just arrived in York.

Tommy And what do you think to the old place?

Colin Well, I haven't had much time to look round yet, but one thing I
have noticed: all the roads seem to be rather bumpy and uneven.

Tommy Oh, I know. They're always digging 'em up round here. First of all
the Council digs 'em up, then the Gas Board digs 'em up, then the
Water Board has a go and the Electricity Board finishes 'em off. It's
got so bad down *our* road, we haven't got a white line down the middle
of it—we've got a zip.

Colin laughs

So what are you doing in York then? You're not selling pegs and bits
of privet hedge, are you?

Colin (*smiling*) As a matter of fact, I'm looking for work. I thought I
might get a job at the Annual Fayre, but it seems that I've arrived on
the wrong day.

Tommy Oh, no you haven't. This is the right day, all right, but the new
High Sheriff's just been here and cancelled the whole thing.

Colin Whatever for?

Tommy Don't ask me. He's just like that. Everybody here thinks he's a
real pain in the neck—except me. I've got a *much* lower opinion of him.

Colin Hmmm. So he's a nasty piece of work, is he? What's his name?

Tommy Baron Snatcher.

Colin (*stunned*) Snatcher? The new High Sheriff of York?

Tommy Yes. Do you know him, then?

Colin (*grimly*) I'll say I know him. He's the scoundrel who had me jailed
at Lincoln a few years ago. He claimed I'd been stealing purses in the
Market Place, but actually, Pye and Peas, his two henchmen were the
real thieves. They shared the stolen money between them and planted
the empty purses on innocent bystanders who were then arrested by the
Baron in order to claim the rewards. That way they all made a very
good living and no-one even suspected them.

Tommy Oooh, the rotten lot.

Colin By the time I'd managed to prove myself innocent, they'd all left
the City, but I vowed that one day I'd get my own back. Perhaps that
day is closer than I think.

Tommy Yes, but just you be careful. He's real sneaky that Baron Snatcher
is. He's the kind of feller that'll pat you on the back to your face, but
the minute you turn round, he'll sock you in the teeth.

Colin Don't worry, I'll deal with him all right. But first of all, I've got to
find somewhere to live. Can you help me?

Tommy Course I can. We'll go and see Martha Muffett. She lives in that cottage over there. (*He points*) She'll be only too pleased to fix you up. Any friend of mine is a friend of hers.

Colin Oh. You know her quite well, do you?

Tommy Know her? (*He laughs*) We're engaged to be married. She's my fiasco.

Colin (*amused*) Surely you mean your *fiancée*?

Tommy I know what I mean. Come on. I'll introduce you.

Colin And you're sure she'll take me in?

Tommy She will if you're not careful.

Tommy and Colin cross to the cottage and enter it. As they do so, Pye and Peas enter L. *They look like comedy thugs from a child's comic paper*

Pye Well. Here we are, Peas . . . and there's the cottage. (*He indicates*)

Peas Good. In you go, Pye. (*He rubs his hands with glee*)

Pye What do you mean, "in I go"? What about you?

Peas Oh, *I* couldn't do it, old chap. You see, *I* know the visiting times and you don't.

Pye Visiting times? What visiting times?

Peas The *hospital* visiting times. I mean—(*he gives a little laugh*)—you'll want someone to come and visit you, won't you?

Pye (*baffled*) I don't get you, Peas. I'm not going into hospital.

Peas Of course you are, dear boy. I shall insist upon it. You can't just lie there in the street with all *your* injuries. It'll be absolute agony for you.

Pye But I haven't got any injuries.

Peas (*patiently*) I know you haven't—yet. But look ahead.

Pye (*worried*) Here—you don't think she's going to cut up rough, do you?

Peas My dear Pye, I'm convinced of it. They don't call her the Fruit Lady for nothing, you know.

Pye Fruit Lady?

Peas Yes. She's as tough as an old pommegranite, slippery as a banana skin, sour as a lemon, and when you try to put the squeeze on her, she'll hit you in the eye like a grapefruit.

Pye (*gulping*) Oh—well, couldn't we leave it for today, Peas? We could always tell the Baron that she wasn't in.

Peas (*frowning*) Do you mean to tell me you're *scared* of her?

Pye Me? Scared? (*He snorts*) Huh. Before I teamed up with you, I used to be in a job where a man had to have plenty of guts.

Peas Ah, yes. I remember. You used to string tennis rackets.

Pye (*annoyed*) No I did not. As a matter of fact, I was a very important person. I had hundreds of people under me, you know.

Peas Of course. You were a watchman at a cemetery.

Pye Oh, it's useless trying to talk to you. You think you're real clever, don't you?

Peas (*modestly*) Well, most people seem to think that I'm a great *wit*.

Pye Yes. Well they're only *half* right.

Peas Do I detect a note of sarcasm in your voice, dear boy? A little touch of . . .

Melody, the Grand Duke's Ward enters UR. *She carries a small purse*

Hello, hello, hello. And what have we here, then?

Pye (*mockingly*) Looks like it's pretty Miss Melody, the Grand Old Duke's ward. (*He leers at her*)

Peas (*moving to one side of her*) And what might *you* be doing in this part of the City, my dear?

Pye (*moving to her other side*) Don't you know it could be *dangerous* to go wandering around York on your ownsome?

Melody (*fearlessly*) It wouldn't be if you two and that crooked master of yours weren't always lurking about. (*She moves* D)

Peas My, my. The girl has spirit. (*He indicates the purse*) And what's that clutched tightly in her dainty little hand, I wonder?

Melody If you *must* know, it's money the Grand Old Duke has sent to Martha to pay the rent she owes.

Pye (*beaming*) In that case, you'd better hand it over to us, and *we'll* see that the Baron gets it. (*He holds out his hand*)

Melody Oh, no. I wouldn't trust you two as far as I could throw you. This goes to Martha or no-one.

Peas We'll see about that. (*To Pye*) Grab her.

Pye grabs hold of Melody and Peas tries to snatch the purse from her

Melody (*struggling*) Help! Help!

Pye It's no use calling for help. There's nobody here to save you.

Peas (*tugging at the purse*) Let go of it.

Melody continues to shout for help

Colin enters from Martha's cottage and sees the struggle

Colin What? (*He dashes over to them*) I'll teach you to attack a helpless girl. Take that! (*He hits Pye*) And that! (*He hits Peas*)

With howls of fright, the two men release Melody and run for their ˙lives, exiting L

Are you all right, miss?

Melody (*smoothing herself down*) Yes, thank you. They were trying to rob me of Martha's rent money. Thank goodness you came along in time to save it.

Colin Not only that. I've managed to save myself some lodgings, too. If Martha isn't going to be turned out, I'll be able to stay with her after all. But allow me to introduce myself. My name is Colin.

Melody And I'm Melody, the Grand Old Duke's ward.

Colin Melody. What a lovely name.

Melody Why, thank you. (*After a pause*) Forgive my asking, but—are you a stranger here? I don't remember seeing you before.

Colin Yes. I've only just arrived. I came to look for work at the Fayre but it seems your new High Sheriff has had it cancelled.

Melody I know, and the Grand Old Duke is furious about it. He's on his way here now to re-open it again. Why he puts up with Baron Snatcher, I can't imagine. A nastier piece of work you could never hope to meet.

Colin Yes. I have met with him before. In fact, I've a little score to settle
with him *and* those two thugs I just chased off, as soon as I get the
chance. But first of all I have to find a job.

Melody That's no problem. I'll ask Uncle Frederick—The Grand Old
Duke, that is—to give you one. Perhaps he'll enlist you in his army?

Colin Me? In the Grand Duke's army? Oh, if only it were possible.

Melody It is. Once I tell him how you saved me. He'll do anything for me.

Colin I'm not surprised. I would myself.

Melody (*laughing*) But you hardly know me.

Colin Perhaps so . . . But somehow I feel as though I've known you all my
life.

Melody Well, now that you come to mention it. I feel the same way about
you.

SONG 4

*After the song, there is a flourish from the trumpets and a rousing March
is heard*

> *The soldiers of the Grand Old Duke arrive, proudly marching in time to
> the music into the Square and positioning themselves at each side of the
> playing area. They are followed by the Grand Old Duke himself, a chubby
> little man with a huge white moustache and dozens of military medals
> pinned to his tunic*

Soldier His Grace . . . The Grand Old Duke of York.

The Duke moves DC

Soldiers (*very loudly*) Hooray!

Duke (*wincing at the blast*) Ooooooooooooooooh! (*He covers his ears*)

Melody (*smiling*) Hello, Uncle Frederick.

Duke (*blinking*) What? (*He clears his ears*) Ah, Melody, my dear. Sorry
we're late, but we took the wrong turning and ended up in the (*local
snack bar*). We couldn't really leave without buying *something*, could
we? The owner would have been *most* upset. But I never realized it took
so long to pour out ten thousand cups of tea.

Melody Never mind. You're here now and that's all that matters. But
where are the rest of the men? You only have one regiment here.

Duke Yes. My faithful Foot and Mouth Brigade. (*He turns and waves to
them*) Oh, I only brought them along in case of emergencies. I've sent
the rest of the army off on a little march. Do you know, I've found
a simply *marvellous* place outside the City walls? I can't think why
we've never used it before. It's a great big hill with absolutely nothing
on it but a few trees and a tumbledown old cottage that looks as though
it hasn't been lived in for years. We can march up and down it for hours
on end without disturbing a soul. As soon as we've finished here, we're
going to join the rest of 'em and march until suppertime. (*Briskly*) Now
then, did you bring the money?

Melody Yes, but I almost lost it. If it hadn't been for Colin, here, the
Baron's henchmen would have stolen it.

Duke (*shocked*) Good Heavens. You mean—there was trouble? (*He looks around nervously*)

Melody I'm afraid so. But don't worry. Colin soon chased them off.

Duke (*mopping his brow*) Thank goodness for that. I couldn't cope with fighting and bloodshed.

Colin (*surprised*) But—I thought you were a famous warrior, Your Grace. A great leader of men.

Melody (*wryly*) I'm afraid he's more like a follower of women.

Colin But what about your reputation as a soldier?

Duke I've got a very good publicity agent. Anyway, I don't want to talk about all *this*. If you saved my little Melody from being robbed, I shall have to reward you, shan't I? What would you like?

Melody Actually, he'd like a job, Uncle Frederick.

Colin (*nodding*) Give me a job in your army, Your Grace. I could go with them into battle and help them fight.

The Soldiers all react with alarm

Duke (*flustered*) Ooooh, now look what you've done. You've upset 'em My soldiers don't *fight*. They're much too delicate.

The Soldiers nod agreement

Colin (*baffled*) Then—what *do* they do if they don't fight?

Duke Well—they march up and down.

The Soldiers nod

Colin And that's all?

Duke (*laughing*) Of course not, you silly boy. The very idea. No, one or two of them knit.

One or two Soldiers produce knitting to show

Melody Well? Will you give him a job, Uncle Frederick?

Duke Oh, I suppose so—providing he doesn't go upsetting the men again. (*To Colin*) How would you like to be a Captain?

Colin (*astounded*) A Captain? *Me* a Captain?

Duke Oh, all right then. A General. I don't care.

Colin (*dazed*) But—but . . . (*Recovering*) Oh, thank you, Your Grace. You won't regret this, I promise you.

Duke (*embarrassed*) Oh, pshaw. It's nothing. (*To Melody*) Now you see that Martha gets her rent money whilst we get back to our marching. We've got to get finished before (*children's TV show*) comes on, you know, or the whole lot of 'em'll be in tears. Bye-bye. (*He shouts*) Troop—quick march!

The March starts up again and the Grand Old Duke and his men exit happily. Colin and Melody wave them good-bye then exit into Martha's cottage. As soon as the Square is empty, Baron Snatcher enters DL, his face grim

Baron So those idiots Pye and Peas were right. It *is* the Gypsy boy from Lincoln, and that dim-witted Duke has taken him into his army. I've got to get rid of him before he can interfere with my plans. Nothing must stand in my way. I intend to be Grand Duke of York if I have to destroy half the City to do it.

There is a tremendous crash of thunder and the Lights turn green as Maleficent, the bad-tempered fairy, enters in a rage

Maleficent (*stamping her foot*) Confound that brainless Duke of York
           And his ten thousand men.
           They march up my Enchanted Hill
           And then march down again.
           Their tramping feet have caused
           My very house to groan and creak;
           If they continue marching
           I'll be homeless in a week.
           The ceiling plaster's cracking
           And a draught is blowing through.
           The chimney shakes with ev'ry step
           And windows break. It's true.
           The floorboards lift at least a foot
           Each time they pass my lane . . .
           It's like living in the flightpath of
           The Concorde aeroplane.
           (*Growing furious*) How *dare* they spoil my peace and quiet?
           I'll have revenge, I swear.
           I'll find a way to make them pay
           I promise you . . .
(*She realizes she is not alone and turns quickly*) Who's there? (*She raises her wand to cast a spell*)

Baron (*terrified*) Ahhhhhhhh! (*He tries to cover his face with his arms*) Who are you?

Maleficent I am the eldest fairy. Maleficent, by name.
           My eyes look deep into your heart and see your little game.
           You scheme against Duke Frederick, and naughty plans
             have made.
           Well, out of *spite*, this very night, your foolish plot I'll aid.

Baron (*gulping*) You will?

Maleficent If you so wish, I'll lend my skills to make your dreams come
            true.
           Duke Frederick shall be destroyed and York belong to *you.*

Baron (*eagerly*) Oh, yes. Yes. Anything you say. (*He fumbles in his pocket*) I've drawn up a little plan, if you'd like to see it . . .

Maleficent (*waving it aside*) Bah. Come to Acomb Woods tonight.
           My plan I'll make quite clear.
           Await me by the blasted oak,
           For that's where I'll appear.

She sniggers and exits L

The Lights return to normal

Baron (*delightedly*) At last things seem to be going my way. With that malicious old harridan helping me out, I'll be Grand Duke of York before the week's over. And who knows, I may even persuade that delicious little Miss Melody to become my Grand Duchess.

He roars with laughter and exits

Mother Shipton enters R

Mother Shipton (*to the audience*) Each character you now have met,
            The good, and evil, too.
            The stage is set. The game's afoot.
            There's no more *I* can do.
            Within the hands of Fate and Chance
            Young Colin's fortune lies.
            From here I can but guide his steps
            And hope his head is wise. (*She raises her wooden spoon*)
            So hear me, Good Dame Fortune, your web begin to
               weave;
            That we may know, and very soon, to laugh and sing—
               or grieve.

Black-out

SCENE 2

A Woody Path in Acomb Woods. Sunset

The Babes or Juniors, dressed as denizens of the wood, perform a dance

At the end of the dance they scurry off as Tommy enters R, *gathering sticks*

Tommy (*to the audience*) Hiya, kids. (*He indicates his sticks*) I'm gathering firewood for old Martha. Since the Grand Old Duke paid her rent money for her, she's decided to cook him something special to show him how grateful she is. (*He laughs*) I'll say it's going to be something special. She's a terrible cook, old Martha is. Can't even boil water without burning it. You know, she's got the only house in York where the mice get food parcels from Oxfam. (*He chuckles*)

Martha enters behind him, gathering sticks

Anyway . . . here we are in Acomb Woods. I don't know where Martha's got to, but I don't suppose she'll be far away. She loves Nature, you know—despite what it did to her.

Martha reacts

Have you ever seen so many wrinkles in one face? If it wasn't for her eyes, nose and mouth, you'd think it was a ploughed field.

Martha's lips set tightly and she moves D

She daren't wear dropped ear-rings. They make her face look like a venetian blind. (*He chortles*) She went to have some photographs taken last month but the photographer hasn't been able to develop 'em yet. He's too scared to go into the darkroom with 'em.

Martha (*grimly*) Oh, he is, is he? (*She drops her sticks and rolls up her sleeves*) Right.

Tommy (*petrified*) Ooooh eck. (*He backs away*) Now Martha—I was only joking.

Martha (*advancing on him*) Oh yes? Well let me see you laugh this off. (*She waves her fist*) Stand still while I hit you.

Tommy (*dodging her*) No, wait. Listen. You don't understand. I knew you were there all the time.

Martha (*scornfully*) Oh, yeah?

Tommy Course I did. You don't think I could let the woman I love come near me without knowing she was there, do you?

Martha Oh—well . . . (*Mollified*) Ooooh, Tommy—do you *really* love me?

Tommy I'll tell you this much for nothing—I didn't realize what happiness was until I got engaged to *you*.

Martha (*delighted*) You didn't? (*To the audience*) Ohhhh did you *hear* that, girls? He didn't realize what happiness was until he got engaged to *me*. (*She simpers and preens*)

Tommy Yes, but by that time it was too late to do anything about it.

Martha (*turning to him*) I say—(*she flutters her lashes at him*)—haven't you noticed anything *different* about me this evening?

Tommy Er—what sort of different, Martha?

Martha Well—(*she caresses her figure*)—I'm wearing my new dress. (*She parades it*) Made it myself out of an old settee cover. It's a good fit, isn't it?

Tommy I don't know about a good *fit*. It looks more like a *convulsion*.

Martha (*pleased*) Flatterer. (*She smirks*) I've called it the "hand grenade" look. Pull one pin out and it's every man for himself. Yippee!

Tommy Martha. Control yourself. Somebody might be listening.

Martha Pooh, I don't care. After all, we have blighted our trough, haven't we? Come on—give me a kiss. (*She grabs hold of him*)

Tommy (*pulling back*) No.

Martha Go on. Go on. (*She purses her lips at him*) Kiss, kiss, kiss.

Tommy (*pulling free*) No.

Martha (*put out*) Why not?

Tommy Well—because I've been hearing some very funny stories about you, Martha Muffett.

Martha (*surprised*) Stories about me? What sort of stories?

Tommy Ones about you flirting with the sailors at Scarborough when you go there for your holidays.

Martha (*scornfully*) Oh, there's nothing wrong in that, you big daft thing. All young girls like the occasional kiss from a nice sailor boy.

Tommy I know. But you've kissed so many, your lips go in and out with the tide. Honestly, Martha, you're *always* kissing other men.

Martha (*indignantly*) I'm certainly not. Since the day you promised to bridalize me, there's only been two occasions when I've been kissed by other men, and I can remember them perfectly. Once I was kissed by the milkman, and the other time I was kissed by the Grand Duke's army. (*She realizes what she has said*) Ooops!

Tommy (*accusingly*) You see?

Martha (*abashed*) Well—(*defensively*)—I can't help having a military heart, can I?

Tommy (*puzzled*) What sort of heart's a military heart?

Martha It's one that's open to all men between the ages of eighteen and forty-five. (*She kicks out her leg with a yell*) Yippee.

Tommy looks put out

Oh, come on. I was only joking. Put your arms around me and call me your little Bluebell. (*She simpers at him*)

Tommy Why should I call you my little Bluebell?

Martha Simple. It's because I grow wild in the woods.

SONG 5

Martha chases Tommy off L after the song

Melody and Colin enter R. Colin is in his new uniform and wears a sword. Unbeknown to them, the Baron, Pye and Peas enter L and immediately hide

Colin (*delightedly*) Oh, Melody. I can't believe it. Me, a poor Gypsy boy, a General in the Grand Duke's army.

Melody (*laughing*) And I must say you look rather dashing in your new uniform.

Colin Why, thank you. But to tell you the truth, I'm not half so concerned about how I look, as I am about finding Baron Snatcher and his henchmen. Since that little episode in the City this morning, no-one's seen a sign of them.

Melody I know. And I don't like it. I'm sure they're up to no good.

Colin Yes, but they'll have a very nasty shock if they try anything whilst *I'm* in York. (*He touches his sword*)

Melody Be careful, Colin.

Colin (*smiling*) Don't worry. If Mother Shipton was telling the truth, I don't think I'm got much to fear from *them*.

Jack and Jill come hurrying in R

Jack Melody. Colin. Thank goodness we found you.

Colin What's wrong?

Jill We were just going to fetch a pail of water for old Dame Dob, when we saw Baron Snatcher and his men slinking into the woods.

Jack They looked so suspicious, we decided to follow them and see what they were up to.

Melody And what was it?

Jill We're not sure, because we lost sight of them about half a mile from here, but we did find *this* on the path. (*She takes a folded paper from her pocket*) One of them must have dropped it.

Jack It's a plan to overthrow the Grand Old Duke and put the Baron in his place.

Colin What? (*He takes the paper and reads it quickly*)

Melody Oh, Colin. We must warn him at once.

Colin (*looking up*) Don't worry, Melody. There isn't much the Baron can do with only two men to help him. I can deal with *them* by myself.

Jack All the same, I think we'd better be getting back to York. As soon as he realizes he's lost his plan, he's bound to come looking for it.

Colin You're right. (*He folds the letter and slips it into his belt*) And if there *is* going to be any fighting, I'd like you all to be somewhere safe before it begins. Come on. I'll take you back to York.

Colin, Melody, Jack and Jill exit R

The Baron, Pye and Peas emerge from hiding L

Baron (*snarling*) Curses. That snivelling Gypsy brat's managed to get hold of my battle-plan. If he shows it to old Frederick, we're sunk. We'll all be in the stocks and I'll never get the chance to overthrow him.

Pye Don't worry, boss. We'll get it back for you.

Peas Leave it to us, old chap.

Baron (*grabbing Peas and almost choking him*) You? You bungling bone-head! It's thanks to you we lost the plan in the first place. Why don't you sew up the holes in your pockets? (*He flings him aside*)

Pye Well . . .

Baron Silence! Now wait here while I go find that bad-tempered old fairy Maleficent. With a bit of luck she'll get rid of the lot of 'em for me without even *using* the plan. Which will be very nice for *me* as it'll save me the expense of paying you two idiots.

The Baron exits L

Peas (*dusting himself down*) Well the nasty old so-and-so. Fancy talking to *us* like that. *And* trying to get out of paying us our wages.

Pye Yeah. He's so miserly, he'd steal dead flies from a blind spider. I've a good mind to go after him and tell him what he can do with his rotten job.

Peas Jolly good idea, Pye. Why don't you?

Pye He might give us the sack.

Peas (*glumly*) Yes. I'm afraid you're right. But we've got to do something about that plan, old bean. If Maleficent doesn't help us we'll be done for.

Pye I know. Let's follow the Gypsy boy and see if we can pick his pocket before he gets to the Grand Old Duke.

Peas Good idea. I do enjoy picking the occasional pocket. After him.

Pye and Peas exit R

Maleficent enters L *in a green light*

Maleficent (*chuckling*) He he. 'Tis like old times
        To interfere with mortal men.
        I thought, in fact, I'd quite retired,

But here I am again.
I've looked through all my spell books
And though *some* are out of date,
There's still a lot of nasty ones
I'm happy to relate. (*She smirks*)
There's one to make the nicest food
Go soggy, dry, or stale . . .
(I've used that one with great success
On British "Hi-speed" Rail)
One more gives "Pop" stars *talent*
(Quite *ruins* their career).
Another makes M.P.s *de*-crease
Their salaries each year.
But still my favourite one of all
(Excuse the nasty smirk)
Is used to torment Union men.
It forces them to *work*. (*She shrieks with laughter*)
Oh, yes, there's lots of wicked things
Still left for me to do.
So best beware, I might just care
To put a spell on *you*. (*She points at someone in the audience and laughs*)

Baron Snatcher enters L

Baron So there you are. Well? What's this little plan of yours?

Maleficent (*snapping*) Watch your tongue, mortal. *I'll* do the sarcastic bits. Draw closer. (*She crooks her finger at him*) There is no time to lose if you would become Grand Duke of York. You must show your hand at once.

Baron You don't mean to tell me you've dragged me all the way out here just to tell my fortune?

Maleficent Fool. You must prepare yourself for battle. Go to Frederick and tell him you intend to reign over York.

Baron (*blinking*) What?

Maleficent Reign over York.

Baron (*annoyed*) Blast . . . and I've left all my washing out.

Maleficent (*fuming*) Dolt. Idiot. Do you want to be Grand Duke of York or don't you?

Baron (*shaken*) Oh—yes. Yes. Of course I do.

Maleficent Then listen. This very night I shall build for you a magic castle overlooking the City. From it you will lead your men against Frederick and *destroy* him.

Baron (*aghast*) Are you out of your tiny little mind? I've only got two men and they couldn't fight their way out of a paper bag.

Maleficent Fear not, for I shall aid them with my magic charms. The Grand Duke's army shall be scattered like leaves in the wind, and by this time tomorrow, *you* will be the new ruler of York. Now come. We have work to do. (*She seizes the Baron's arm and pulls him away*)

Mother Shipton enters R *and watches Maleficent and the Baron exit* L.
The Lights return to normal

Mother Shipton There go two nasty bits of work—and *both* on mischief
                    bound.
                    My duties now I mustn't shirk. Young Colin must be
                    found.
                    It looks as though he'll need *my* help if York is not to
                    fall;
                    So come, let's haste to join him at the Duke's ancestral
                    hall.

She waves her wooden spoon and there is Black-out

SCENE 3

*A Large Hall inside the Mansion House of the Grand Old Duke. Around the
walls are suits of armour, various campaign flags and portraits of the Grand
Old Duke's ancestors*

*As the Lights come up the Servants are sweeping, polishing, dusting etc., and
singing happily as they work*

SONG 6

At the end of the song they exit in a flurry

Colin and Melody enter R, *the battle-plan still tucked inside Colin's belt*

Melody You wait here, and I'll see if I can find Uncle Frederick.

Colin (*nodding*) The sooner he sees this, the better. (*He pats the plan*)

Melody You—you don't think there's any chance that Baron Snatcher
will manage to overthrow him, do you?

Colin (*laughing*) Not with *this* plan, I don't. It's the most childish plan
I've ever seen.

Melody (*brightening*) Then if there's no *real* danger, why bother to show
it to Uncle Frederick at all?

Colin Because it'll prove to him once and for all that Baron Snatcher
isn't to be trusted. With any luck, he'll order the old crook to leave the
City at once, and *that* wouldn't be bad news for anyone, would it?

Melody Except the Baron and his henchmen. (*She laughs*) I'll be back in a
moment.

Melody exits L

Colin (*cock-a-hoop*) I *said* I'd get even with him somehow, and this looks
like the perfect opportunity. By tomorrow evening all three of them
will be halfway across the country, looking for somewhere to hide their
ugly faces.

Mother Shipton enters R

Mother Shipton Don't count your chicks before they're hatched

My fine young soldier boy.
Before that villain you despatch
There'll be an end to joy.
I come to give you warning fair. Disaster soon befalls.
Before tomorrow evening's out, down will fall York's
        wooden walls.

Colin (*startled*) What?

Mother Shipton The sharp-tongued fay, Maleficent, has vowed to help
        his cause;
        And Frederick, with all his men, is helpless 'gainst *her*
        claws.

Colin (*stunned*) In that case we don't stand a chance. How can we fight
against magic? Unless *you* can help us.

Mother Shipton Alas, no magic pow'rs have I, but only second sight.
        Your skill and brains and courage, will have to win
        this fight.
        But fear you not. I'll do my best to show the path to
        tread.
        As for the outcome—for the nonce—it rests within my
        head.

She taps her temple with her finger and exits

Colin (*calling*) Wait . . .

Melody enters L

Melody He'll be down in a few moments. He's just making Horlicks for
the soldiers. (*She notices Colin's face*) Is something wrong?

Colin (*noticing her*) I've just seen Mother Shipton again. She says that
Baron Snatcher has asked a fairy named Maleficent to help him overthrow your uncle.

Melody (*aghast*) Maleficent?

Colin Do you know of her?

Melody (*worried*) Everyone in Yorkshire knows of her. Oh, Colin. What
are we going to do?

Colin (*putting his arm around her*) Let her poke her nose into things while
I'm around, and I'll show you.

Melody But you don't understand. Maleficent is centuries old, and her
powers are frightening. (*She turns away from him very distressed*)

Colin So what? Fairy or no fairy, we can't just stand by and let her help
Baron Snatcher defeat your uncle without at least *trying* to fight back.
(*He rests his hands on her shoulders*)

*Pye and Peas enter cautiously behind them. Pye spots the plan and indicates
it to Peas*

Melody I suppose you're right. (*She tries to smile*) And if we have to go
into battle, I'm glad to know that *you'll* be leading the men instead of
Uncle Frederick.

Colin Only if he *agrees* to my leading them.

Melody Oh, I'm sure he will. He's a darling, but he hasn't the faintest idea of fighting. Without you we'd be certain to lose.

Colin We won't. I promise you.

Melody What makes you so certain?

Colin Because I've got something worth fighting for—you. And when the battle's over and the enemy defeated, I'll come to claim your hand in marriage as my sole reward.

Melody (*smiling*) And never will a reward be given so gladly.

SONG 7

As Melody and Colin sing Peas creeps down to Colin and steals the plan from his belt

Pye and Peas exit R *triumphantly*

At the end of the song Colin and Melody exit L *holding hands*

As they leave Martha and Tommy enter R. *Martha is resplendant in an outrageous gown*

Tommy (*to the audience*) Hiya, kids.

Martha (*to the audience*) Do you like it, girls? (*She parades the dress*) I call it my "barbed-wire" dress. It protects the property, but doesn't conceal the view.

Tommy Oh, never mind about your dress, Martha. We've come here to thank Duke Frederick for paying your rent money, not to give a fashion show.

Martha (*pushing him*) Listen, cloth-ears. I haven't set foot in this place for nearly twenty years, and I want to make a good impression. Now remember, just watch your manners when you meet his Dukefulness, and if your nose starts running again, don't sniffle. Use what nature provided—your sleeve.

Tommy Oh, Martha. You don't have to keep telling me what to do. I have been to Court before, you know.

Martha Yes. The Magistrates Court.

Tommy No. It was *real* Royalty. Honest.

Martha Listen, pop-eyes. The only Royalty you've ever been connected with is *The Queen's Arms*, *The King's Head* and *The Crown Hotel*.

Tommy Oh, well, if you're going to be rotten to me, I might as well go home again. Why can't you be nice, for a change?

Martha And what do you think I've been doing for the last twenty years? If it hadn't been for *me*, what would you have been now?

Tommy Happy.

Martha hits him with his own cap

Owwwwwwwwwwwww!

Martha (*tossing the cap aside; worried*) Ooooh, I wonder if I should have worn my other dress?

Tommy (*recovering his cap*) *Which* other dress?

Martha My "Atomic Bomb" dress, of course. (*To the audience*) It's got a ninety per cent fall out. (*Enthusing*) Oooooh, you should see it, girls. I look as though I've been poured into it and I forgot to say "when". Mind you, I do have to watch meself when I'm wearing it. I keep getting me foot caught in the neckline.

Tommy Never mind your neckline. Let's go find the Grand Old Duke.

Martha Wait a minute. *Wait* a minute. (*To the audience*) He has to do everything in a *rush*. (*To Tommy*) Give me a bit of time to pull meself together. I want to get rid of this headache before I meet him again, anyway.

Tommy Oh—I'm sorry, Martha. I didn't realize you had a headache.

Martha Well of course I've got a headache. It's all the excitement and rushing around. The thought of seeing old Freddie again after all these years. I mean—if it hadn't been for that, I wouldn't have had a milk bath in the first place, and if I hadn't had the milk bath, I wouldn't have given meself a headache.

Tommy (*puzzled*) How can a milk bath give you a headache?

Martha The cow slipped and fell on top of me. (*She looks round*) Ohhhh. Look at this place. Doesn't it bring back memories?

Tommy How do you mean?

Martha Well, I only have to glance around this hall and it happens. A wave of neuralgia sweeps over me. What a history this place has. Built over five hundred years ago, and in all that time not a thing has been altered, not a stone has been touched and not a fragment of its framework has been replaced.

Tommy Blimey. The Old Duke must have the same landlord as me.

Martha (*peeved*) Oh, shurrup, useless. (*She pushes him*) Ah, well ... I suppose I'd better go and get it over with. (*She begins to move* L, *then pauses*) Here—I've just thought on. As soon as I've thanked Frederick for the rent money, let's get married to celebrate.

Tommy Eh?

Martha We can go to Scotland for our honeymoon and I'll let you wear my late husband's kilt.

Tommy Oh, I couldn't wear a kilt, Martha. I'd be too embarrassed.

Martha No you wouldn't. Everybody wears kilts in Scotland. That's why they're always smiling.

Tommy How do you work that out?

Martha It's an old Scottish motto. (*She recites*)
Up there in Bonnie Scotland
No matter what the weather ...
You'll always see Scots with a smile on their face.
It's a case of short kilts and long heather.

Tommy Well—have you still got it, then? Your late husband's kilt?

Martha I certainly have. He sold it to me on his deathbed. (*She sniffles*) Every time I look at it, I think of how he looked on our wedding day.

Tommy Tall, dark and handsome?

Martha (*shaking her head*) Paralytic. Still—we had a real Scottish wedding, you know.

Tommy Married over the anvil at Gretna Green?

Martha No. The confetti was on elastic. (*To the audience*) Oh, girls. You should have seen it. It was ever such a posh do. We even had a real brass band. He slipped it on to me finger during the ceremony. Mind you, I couldn't grumble. He didn't have much money, poor love. Two other Scotsmen made him bankrupt.

Tommy Who were they?

Martha Haig and Johnny Walker. (*She sobs*) Poor little Gherkin.

Tommy *Gherkin?*

Martha I called him that because he was always pickled. (*She sniffles*) And it was the drink that finished him off, too. He fell into a vat of pure malt whisky. Took him four days to drown. (*She sobs*)

Tommy Four days?

Martha (*nodding*) He kept getting out to go to the toilet.

The Baron enters R *followed by Pye and Peas*

Baron (*spotting Tommy and Martha*) Ahaaaaaa! (*He advances on them*)

Tommy Look out. Here comes the best-known sculptur in the district.

Baron (*snarling*) And what's *that* supposed to mean?

Tommy York's biggest chiseller.

Baron (*snorting*) Bah! (*To Pye and Peas*) Arrest these two idiots and throw them into the dungeons!

Pye and Peas pounce on Tommy and Martha and a struggle begins with lots of shouting

Servants, Soldiers and Jack and Jill hurry in

Servants (*with voices overlapping*) What's happening? What's wrong? Etc.

Martha (*tearfully*) We've been arresticated. Run in, and about to be run out.

Servants and Soldiers (*to the Baron and his men*) Boo! Hiss! Shame! Etc.

Baron (*loudly*) Silence. These miserable villains crept in here tonight to help that treacherous Gypsy boy, Colin, overthrow the Grand Old Duke.

The Servants and Soldiers react in astonishment

(*Smirking*) Luckily *I* found out about it in time and managed to collar them before any damage was done. All we have to do now is capture the Gypsy, and the whole lot of 'em can rot in my dungeons.

Jack (*stepping forward*) Rubbish. If anyone's trying to overthrow the Grand Old Duke, it's you.

Jill Yes. *We* know all about your secret battle-plan.

Baron (*innocently*) Which secret battle-plan?

Colin, Melody and the Grand Old Duke enter

Colin The one I have here in my belt, you old villain. Found by Jack and Jill in the woods and written in your own handwriting.

Everyone reacts

Baron (*sneering*) A likely story. (*He points at Colin*) Arrest that boy at once!

Two Soldiers move towards Colin

Colin Wait. Take a look at this first. (*He puts his hand to his belt for the plan*) It will prove to all of you just what a—*it's gone.*

Baron (*triumphantly*) You see? To the dungeons with him—and take this lot as well.

The Soldiers seize Colin, Jack and Jill

Colin (*struggling*) No. You're making a mistake.

Baron (*sneering*) The only mistake that's been made around here, Gypsy boy, was the one *you* made when you tried to get the better of *me.* (*To the Duke*) These so called battle-plans never existed at all, Your Grace. It was just a trick to wheedle his way into your good books and then destroy you.

Melody It *wasn't*, Uncle Frederick. I saw the plans myself.

Duke (*flustered*) Oh, dear. This is all very difficult. (*To the Baron*) You see—I've just been told that *you* were plotting to overthrow me. You want to take my place.

Pye That's a lie. He never eats plaice. Cod's *his* favourite.

Duke Is it true?

Baron Of course it is. I detest plaice.

Duke No, no. I meant is there a plot afoot to bump me off?

Baron (*in mock amazement*) Bump you off? How can Your Grace think such things? You know *I'd* never lift a finger to harm you.

Melody Don't listen to him, Uncle Frederick. He's lying.

Baron Oh, no I'm not.

Audience participation

Duke (*more flustered*) Oh, I don't know *who* to believe.

Tommy Well, I wouldn't believe old Snatcher if I were you. He tells more lies than the weather forecasters.

Baron (*snarling*) How dare you? Ask anybody here. They'll tell you I've been *married* to the truth since childhood. (*He preens*)

Martha (*pulling free*) Izzat so? Well I've got news for you, mate. Your divorce has just come through. (*She marches down to him*) You can't even *tell* the truth without lying about it.

Duke (*recognizing her*) Martha . . . my old nurserymaid.

Martha (*slightly embarrassed*) Hello, Freddie.

Duke (*embracing her warmly*) What on earth are you doing here? After all these years.

Martha We just popped in to say thank you for sending that rent money, and that great gorilla—(*indicating the Baron*)—set his two pet fleas on to us. He was going to throw us into his dungeons.

Duke Nonsense. (*To the Baron*) How dare you lay hands on my poor little Martha?

Baron (*taken aback*) But you don't understand. She and the Gypsy boy are in league with the others. Until they're under lock and key you're in terrible danger.

Colin Rubbish. He *is* trying to overthrow you, and if only I had that plan I could prove it to you.

Pye (*smirking*) But you haven't got the plan, have you?

Peas Because *we* managed to steal it back again without you noticing. (*He preens himself*)

Everyone reacts. Peas realizes what he has said

Martha⎫
Tommy⎬ *together* ⎨ Ahaaaaaaaa!

Baron (*to Peas*) You *fool*! You've given the game away. Run for it.

Colin (*pulling free*) Stop them!

The Baron, Pye and Peas dash off chased by the Servants and Soldiers

Melody runs to Colin and embraces him. Jack hugs Jill and Martha hugs Tommy

Jack (*laughing*) I don't think we'll have any more trouble with those three.

Jill I've never seen anyone so anxious to leave the City.

Duke (*indignantly*) And to think I actually *trusted* that scoundrel. Gave him a free hand.

Martha That's the trouble with giving folks like him a free hand. They usually go sticking it into other people's pockets.

Duke Anyway—(*brightening*)—we're well rid of the lot of 'em. He won't dare show his face around here again. I think this is the perfect opportunity to have a little celebration party.

Melody Oh, but we can't, Uncle. Not yet.

Colin We're in more trouble than we thought. You see, the Baron had asked the bad-tempered fairy Maleficent to help him—and she's promised to do so.

Everyone reacts

Duke (*quaking*) Maleficent? But—but—how could he? I mean—I thought she was dead.

There is a crash of thunder

Maleficent appears L and the Lights go green

Maleficent Dead? Dead? You thought I was *dead*?
Whatever put thoughts like *that* in your head?
I'm *very* alive. Wicked, cunning and clever . . .
With heart black as night and bad-tempered as ever.

Duke (*nibbling at his fingernails*) W—w—w—what do you want? W—w—w—what are you doing here?

Maleficent (*annoyed*) What do I want? You milit'ry *mouse*.
I'm seeking revenge for the loss of my house.
Your idiot army has marched up and down
My Enchanted Hill hourly—from foot unto crown.
And with the vibration, my cottage so sweet

Now lies there in *ruins*. I'm out in the street.
I haven't a roof o'er my head to give cover,
And I'll have to get Wimpey's to build me another.
Duke Oh, dear.
Maleficent So there now you have it. From this moment on
Your fortunes are fading and soon will be gone.
Your army I'll scatter—York's great walls shall fall—
And there'll be, by tomorrow, an end to you *all*. (*She cackles*)

All react in consternation

Colin Wait. What if we promise to build you another house, ourselves?
Even better than the one you lost? Will you change your mind?
Maleficent Change my mind? *Never*. The question's absurd.
To bad Baron Snatcher I've given my word.
I'll help him destroy the Grand Duke, out of spite.
So until we next meet on the morrow . . . Goodnight.

There is a crash of thunder and she exits. The Lights return to normal

Martha That's torn it.
Tommy What are we going to do now?
Jack We don't stand a chance.
Jill It's the end for us all. (*She clings on to Jack*)
Duke (*dismayed*) It's all my fault too. How could *I* know she lived on
that silly old hill?
Melody (*trying to comfort him*) It couldn't be helped, Uncle Frederick.
Colin (*brightly*) Well, what a miserable set of faces. Come on. Cheer up.
We're not beaten yet. Maleficent may have magic powers, but *we've*
got brains and courage—not to mention an army of ten thousand men.
If it's a fight she wants, then let's give her one. Arm yourselves with
anything you can lay your hands on and meet me in the City Square
as soon as it's daylight.

Martha, Tommy, Jack, Jill and the Duke exit quickly

Melody and Colin begin to move away and the Lights start to fade

Melody (*worried*) Do you think we stand any chance at all. Colin?
Colin (*drawing his sword*) I don't know, Melody—but we'll soon find out.

They exit and the Lights fade quickly to Black-out

SCENE 4

Down Whip-ma Whop-ma Lane. A street of half-timbered houses

*Babes or Juniors enter dressed as toy soldiers and perform a dance routine
to music*

At the end of the routine Black-out

S<small>CENE</small> 5

The City Square. Early morning half-light

> *A Watchman enters* R, *carrying a lantern. He moves leisurely across the stage calling loudly*

Watchman Seven o'clock in the morning and all's well.

> *He repeats this at intervals before, finally he exits* L. *His voice fades gradually*

> *The Baron, Pye and Peas enter* R *furtively. In single file they move* C, *the Baron looking ahead and Pye and Peas to each side and behind them*

The Baron suddenly stops dead in his tracks and the others cannon into him. All yell in panic

Baron (*furiously*) Shhhh!

Peas (*to Pye*) Shhhhhh!

Pye (*to the space behind him*) Shhhh. (*He realizes no-one is there*)

Baron (*snarling*) Why don't you watch where you're going, you bungling, brainless baboons?

Peas I say, old chap. Steady on. You were the one who stopped.

Pye Yes. Why don't you give some hand signals?

Baron (*with anguish*) Shhhhhhhh!

Peas (*to Pye*) Shhhhhh!

Pye (*to the space behind him*) Shhhhhh! (*He realizes again*)

Baron (*pulling them in*) Now then. We've got to get out of the City before they discover us. I don't fancy another night in that pigsty.

Peas Me neither. But how are we going to manage it, old sport? The gates won't be opened at all today, and the streets'll be crawling with soldiers looking for us.

Pye So what? Once old Fairy Whatsername gets busy, we won't have a thing to worry about.

Baron (*snarling*) We will if she doesn't turn up like she promised. We'll be stuck in the dungeons for the next fifty years. (*He peers round*) If only I knew where the old faggot was.

Peas If you ask me, *I* think she's done a bunk. She's realized she's bitten off more than she can chew, and hopped it.

Pye Yeah. The Duke's ten thousand men have scared her off.

> *There is a crash of thunder and Maleficent appears in a green Light*

Malecfient So—you think I'd run away and hide in fear of mortal foe?
Then let me just remind you of a fact you *all* should know.
Whenever *I* have made a vow, that promise has been kept.
  (*She points* L)
Look now upon the work *I've* done whilst fools like you
  have slept.

Baron (*looking off* L) It's a *castle*. On top of the hill.

Pye and Peas goggle

Maleficent As grim as death. As strong as steel, your magic castle
                    stands.
                    So come. I'll take you there until the City's in your hands.
Baron (*anxiously*) Wait. What about all my gold and things? I can't leave
    them here. Someone dishonest might nick 'em.
Maleficent (*snarling*) What do *I* care about your trinkets? *Quickly.* (*She
    turns to exit*)
Baron Trinkets? There's a lifetime of *fiddles* gone into collecting those
    things. I could pay off the National Debt with it.
Maleficent Very well. Collect what you can, but hurry. I'll return in a few
    minutes, but keep me waiting and I promise you, you'll be on your own.
    Do you understand?

She exits quickly, and the Lights return to normal

Baron (*to Pye and Peas*) Quick. Back to Seizitt Hall.

The Baron, Pye and Peas hurry off

Colin, Melody and the Duke enter

Colin Now has everything been done that I requested, Your Grace?
Duke (*miserably*) Yes—but what's the use? We haven't a chance.
Melody Of course we have, Uncle Frederick. With Colin in charge of the
    men we can't possibly lose the battle.
Duke (*cheering up*) Are you sure?
Colin Positive. Now, are all the City gates barred?

The Duke nods

    And there's a regiment of soldiers at each gateway?

The Duke nods again

    And what weapons are they carrying?
Duke Well—I know *one* man has a *pea-shooter*.

Colin glances uneasily at Melody

Colin What about the others?
Duke (*timidly*) First-aid boxes in case he faints.
Melody (*disappointedly*) Uncle.
Duke (*almost in tears*) I'm sorry, Melody, but you know how we feel
    about fighting. We'd much sooner chase butterflies.
Colin But Your Grace—think about the great warriors of the past. I'm
    sure *they* didn't like the idea of fighting, but they did it just the same.
    They did it for Britain . . . for Freedom . . . for Justice.
Duke They did?

Colin and Melody nod

    Er—who, for instance?
Colin Well—er—Admiral Lord Nelson, for one.

Duke Oh—I've heard of *him*. Didn't he fight the battle of Trafalgar?

Melody (*delightedly*) That's right, Uncle.

Duke Ah, *Trafalgar*. I can picture it now. (*Enthusing*) What a sight it must have been. All those gallant British ships . . . side by side . . . guns blazing at the enemy.

Melody The billowing white sails and crashing waves.

Colin Hand to hand fighting. The smoke . . . the shouting and screaming . . . swords flashing in the sunlight.

Duke (*getting carried away*) Cannonballs zooming all over the place. The R.A.F. dropping bombs. John Wayne leading the U.S. Cavalry . . . Oooooh, I wish I could have been there. (*He blinks*) Just a minute, though. I don't understand. How on earth did they manage to get all that lot into Trafalgar Square? That silly stone column takes up most of the room.

Colin No, no, Your Grace. Nelson didn't fight in Trafalgar *Square*.

Duke I know he didn't. Sensible fellow. He stood on top of that column and watched the others do it for him.

Melody No, Uncle. You don't understand. The battle wasn't anywhere *near* Trafalgar Square. It took place hundreds of miles away from there.

Duke (*daylight dawning*) Ohhhhh, I see. (*He laughs*) Silly old me. Of course. That explains why he needed the *telescope*. I've often wondered about that, you know. Well, well, well.

Colin and Melody admit defeat

Colin It's no use, Your Grace. I don't think you'll ever be able to understand. You seem to have no grasp of military tactics at all.

Duke Oh, but you're wrong. I *do*. I've got a very *good* grasp of them—thanks to my noble ancestor the Duke of Plaza-Toro. Did I ever tell you about him? No? Then I'll do it now.

SONG 8

As the Duke sings the sky begins to lighten gradually until the Lights come up to full

At the end of the song, Jack and Jill enter armed with a sword and saucepan respectively

Jack (*excitedly*) Your Grace. Colin. Look. (*He points off* L)

Jill It's a huge black castle. It appeared in the night like magic.

Colin (*grimly*) It *was* magic. This is obviously Maleficent's work. She must be getting ready to launch her attack on us.

Duke (*his nerves breaking*) Ooo-er. (*He scuttles* R *as if to exit*)

Melody (*calling*) Uncle Frederick. Where are you going?

Duke (*stopping*) I—er—I've just remembered I haven't seen Aunt Ernestine in New Zealand, lately. There's just time to catch the next plane out there.

Colin But you can't leave *now*, Your Grace. You have to give the troops your address.

Duke Oh, it doesn't matter about that. I shan't expect them to write to me.

Melody No, no, Uncle. He means you have to make a speech to them.

Jack To give them courage before the fighting starts.

Duke (*weakly*) I wish someone would make a speech to *me*.

Jill Shall I go see if they're starting to gather?

Martha and Tommy enter in "cod" military gear and carrying weapons

Martha Don't bother. They are. They're gathering their things together and packing their bags. (*To the Duke*) Do something, Frederick.

Colin Don't worry, Martha. We'll stop them. Come on, Melody.

Melody and Colin hurry off

Tommy (*to the audience*) Hiya, kids. (*Audience reaction*) Well—it looks like this is it, folks. It's us against them.

Martha Here—here. Will you stop talking to that lot and consecrate on what's going on up here. And wipe that smile off your face, as well. This is deadly serious, this is.

Tommy Well, I'm sorry, Martha, but you know what they say. A man's gotta do what a man's gotta do. (*He swaggers* D *like John Wayne*)

Martha (*grimly*) Yes—and a woman's gotta do what a woman's gotta do—and that's clobber you round the earhole if you don't start behaving yourself.

Tommy Oh, you can mock, Martha Muffett—but just let me get my hands on old Snatcher and Co, and by this time tomorrow I could be a Court Martial.

Martha You're more likely to be a General Nuisance. Still—you have got the right idea. You fix old Snatcher, and I'll settle with that Maleficent woman. (*She waves her weapon*) I'll hit her on the nose so hard with this, she'll be breathing through the back of her neck for a month.

Jack That's the spirit, Martha. If only the Grand Duke's soldiers had your determination, we'd be home and dry.

Martha (*modestly*) Oh, well—I suppose that's where my military experience shows through, isn't it?

Jill Military experience? You mean—you once served in the army?

Martha I certainly did. I was Frederick's first woman soldier, wasn't I Freddie?

Duke Eh? What? (*He remembers*) Oh, yes. Yes. But you were also the *last* as I remember.

Tommy Oh, why was that?

Martha (*wryly*) Well, when I first joined up, he told me I'd have to mess with the men, and I was in six months before I found out he meant I'd to *eat* with them.

Colin and Melody enter leading the Soldiers who are arranged so that from an audience point of view, presumably only a portion of them can be seen. The rest are imagined to be off stage. Colin and Melody move down C, *and the rest of the principals down* R

Colin (*loudly*) Men of York. The Grand Old Duke wishes to say something
   to you. (*He steps aside to let the Duke speak*)
Melody (*extending her hand to the Duke*) Come on, Uncle. Say something.
Duke (*weakly*) Hello. (*He gives them a little wave*)
Soldiers (*waving back*) Yoo-hoo. (*They blow kisses, etc.*)
Melody (*urgently*) Make a *speech*.
Duke (*flustered*) Oh—er—yes—of course. Yes. (*He clears his throat*)
   Ahem. (*Loudly*) Friends, Yeomen, Infantrymen. Lend me your spears . . .
Tommy Here, *that* sounds familiar.
Duke Today—*now*, that is—at this moment in time . . . It gives me great
   pleasure—well, no—not exactly *pleasure* . . . More in the way of—er—
   er—er . . . (*He stops and looks helplessly at Colin*)
Colin (*stepping forward*) What the Grand Duke is trying to tell you is that
   today is the day you've all been waiting for.
Soldiers Hooray.

There is general celebration

Jill (*baffled*) What's happening?
Duke They think he means it's the day of the annual picnic.
Colin (*loudly*) It's the day we all go into *battle*. For a fight to the death.

There is an instant silence, then the Soldiers begin to faint

Martha Here—I didn't know this was a passing-out parade.
Duke (*distressed*) There, I *knew* he'd go and upset them. (*He rushes up to
   the Soldiers to comfort them*)
Tommy Upset 'em? I know what I'd do if that lot were anything to do
   with me. I'd plant 'em up to their ankles in concrete—head first.
Jack What are we going to do? It's hopeless trying to fight Maleficent
   with this lot.
Melody But what else can we do? They're all we have.
Colin Unless we can get the Grand Duke to rally them somehow, we'll
   have to do the fighting on our own.
Jill Oh, Martha, can't *you* persuade him to try?
Martha Leave it to me. I'll use my fatal charm on him. Coax him, tempt
   him, and lure him with sweet words.
Tommy But what if *that* doesn't work?
Martha I'll break his flipping neck. (*She makes to go towards the Duke*)

   *Baron Snatcher, Pye and Peas come staggering in under large boxes that
   obstruct their vision. As all watch them, they stagger* C

Baron We're almost there. Hurry. Hurry.
Pye (*panting*) We're going as quick as we can. These boxes weigh a ton.
Peas And I can't even see where I'm going, old chap.

*Colin, Jack and Tommy each lift the top box of a pile and lower them to the
ground*

   That's better . . .

*The villains suddenly realize their position and let out yells. The boxes fall
to the floor and they huddle back to back*

Martha (*grimly*) Well, well, well. If it isn't the three wise monkeys.

Colin and Jack draw their swords

Colin Just the men we're looking for.
Baron (*falling to his knees*) Spare me. I'm too beautiful to die. (*He points to Pye and Peas*) It was all their fault.
Pye
Peas } (*together*) { Mercy. (*They drop to their knees also*)
Jack (*laughing*) Looks like the enemy have surrendered already.

The Soldiers recover rapidly

Duke (*brightening*) You mean we've *won*?
Colin I think we can say that. With these three in our hands, I can't see Maleficent doing battle on her own, can you?

There is a crash of thunder and Maleficent appears in her green light

Maleficent Indeed? Then how surprised you'll be
                    To hear me claim my victory;
                    And with my magic pow'rs to call
                    On wooden walls of York to *fall*.

She gives a flourish of her wand. The Lights flicker and a great crash is heard. All react in horror

                    Where is your shield against me now,
                    O Duke of York? 'Tis gone, I vow;
                    And very soon, when you are dead,
                    Yon grovelling fool—(*indicating the Baron*)—shall rule instead.

There is general reaction. The Baron and his men rise

Colin (*advancing on Maleficent*) Don't be too sure of that, madame.

Maleficent makes a sign and everyone drops their weapons as though they were red hot

Maleficent (*sharply*) My quarrel boy, is not with you . . .
                    But as you wish to join in too,
                    So be it, then—it is my will
                    That *all* but *these*—(*indicating the Baron, Pye and Peas*)—
                        march up that hill.
                    Right to the very top and then
                    Turn round and march back down again.
                    Up and down through night and day.
                    Down and up with no delay.
                    No time to pause, to eat, to drink,
                    No time to talk, no time to think.
                    Time for naught, but marching still
                    Up and down the magic hill.
                    March and do not dare to stop,
                    For when you do, and bodies drop

        Exhausted to the very bone,
        You'll rest forever—*turned to stone.*
Melody (*horrified*) Oh, no. *No.*
Maleficent (*loudly*) O leathered shoes, at my command,
        Begin your march. You understand. (*She points her wand at
            their feet*)
Colin (*firmly*) Stand still, everyone. Don't move a step.

*Against their will, everyone's feet begin to march, slowly at first but gaining
speed*

Martha (*clinging to Tommy as her feet work madly*) Woaaaa! Slow down.
Duke (*loudly*) Stop. Stop, everyone. I *forbid* you to march.
Maleficent Faster, faster. Show who's master.

*The marchers pick up speed, and as they march on the spot, music is blended
in with the beat*

Melody Somebody help us.
Maleficent And now the new Grand Duke and I
        Bid fond farewells.
Baron (*smirking*) Good luck.
Pye
Peas } (*together*){ Bye-bye.

*With a lurch the marchers begin to move off, all calling for help and trying
to stop themselves, as the Baron, Pye, Peas and Maleficent stand jeering at
them*

    *The marchers exit and the music builds to a climax as their voices grow
    fainter*

Baron (*moving down* c *in triumph*) At last, at last. York is in my hands.
    Three cheers for the new Grand Duke. Hip hip——
Pye
Peas } (*together*){ —hooray!

Pye and Peas kneel to the Baron whilst Maleficent shakes with laughter as—

                the CURTAIN *falls*

ACT II

Scene 1

Halfway up the Enchanted Hill

A clearing on a wooded hillside. There are trees L *and* R *and a campfire down extreme* R, *over which is suspended a cauldron which an old Gypsy woman is attending.* DL *a male Gypsy is repairing a heap of shoes. The rest of the Gypsies are singing and dancing in the moonlight*

SONG 9

As the song ends there is commotion from the Gypsies as armed Guards, enter the clearing, followed by Baron Snatcher in his new robes of office, and Pye and Peas

The Baron swaggers DC

Baron So—singing and dancing in defiance of my orders, are you? Not to mention trespassing on my private property. (*To the Guards*) Arrest the lot of 'em.

The Gypsies react as the Guards swoop

1st Gypsy Just a minute. We know of no order forbidding us to enjoy ourselves. And since when has this hillside been owned by you, my friend?

Baron (*snarling*) I'm not your friend, you grubby little peg seller, and for your information, I own every piece of land for as far as the eye can see.

2nd Gypsy (*laughing*) We may only be poor Gypsy folk, but we're not fools. These lands have been the property of the Grand Dukes of York for as long as men can remember. Our people have always been welcome to camp on them.

The Gypsies agree

Baron Oh they have, have they? (*He snarls*) Well they're not welcome *now*. As the *new* Grand Duke of York, I'm in charge of things from now on, and I'm having no petty, pilfering pickpockets parading themselves through *my* City. Understand?

3rd Gypsy (*bewildered*) The *new* Grand Duke? But what's happened to the old one? Duke Frederick?

Baron (*laughing scornfully*) That doddering, old fool? Why, he's dead of course. Him *and* his ten thousand men. Turned to stone by fairy magic and scattered all over this hillside.

The Gypsies react in shock

Away with them.

The Guards begin to drive the Gypsies off

4th Gypsy (*protesting*) What about our property? The trinkets and shoes we are making? (*He indicates the goods*)

Baron (*sneering*) Bah! Filthy rubbish. Leave it where it is. (*He beams*) We can charge you with littering up the countryside, too.

The Gypsies are herded off by the Guards

Baron (*smirking*) That'll show 'em who's boss. (*He kicks the shoes*)

Pye (*worried*) Here—you don't think you were a bit too hard on them, do you? After all, it's not as though they were doing anything wrong.

Baron Are you out of your tiny little mind? Of course they were doing wrong. They're *Gypsies*, aren't they?

Pye Yeah, but all the same—if any of 'em escape they might come looking for revenge.

Baron Bah. And what could they do against *me*? As Grand Duke of York I could order Maleficent to get rid of them for me just like *that*. (*He attempts to snap his fingers but fails. He scowls with embarrassment*)

Peas That's all very well, old chap, but I'd still watch out if I were you. That tall Gypsy looked at you as though *you* were a dirty kitchen floor and *he* were a packet of Flash.

Baron Oh, shut up about the Gypsies and start searching. I want to find that lump of rock that used to be Duke Frederick, and smash it into a thousand pieces.

Pye What for?

Baron I'm taking no chances on somebody breaking the spell and bringing him back to life again. Now move—and if you don't find him before sunrise, I'll stop your wages for the next ten years. I'm going to have a little snooze over there whilst you get on with it.

The Baron exits

Pye (*disgusted*) Huh. Trust old Laundryman. We do all the work and he goes for a lie down.

Peas Yes. And even if we *do* find old Frederick, what will *we* get out of it? Nothing. As usual. (*Puzzled*) By the way—why did you call him "old Laundryman"?

Pye Simple. He'd take the shirt off your back. (*Sourly*) The rotten skinflint. He hasn't even paid us for getting his crackpot battle-plan back, yet. If it hadn't been for us, he'd be sitting in the stocks by now, and Duke Frederick would still be running the City.

Peas You know, I do believe you're right.

Pye So what are we going to do about it?

Peas Well, I know what I'm going to do. I'm going to tell the old miser that if he doesn't give me a rise in wages, I'm handing in my resignation. If he wants his dirty work done in future, he'll have to get it done by a half-wit like you. (*He begins to exit* L)

Pye (*enthusiastically*) Good idea. (*He realizes*) Here—who are you calling a half-wit? I happen to be a man of rare intelligence.

Peas Yes. It's very rare when you show any. My dear Pye, *you* are so stupid, you think Royal Enfield is where the Queen keeps her chickens.

Pye Oh, yes?

Peas Yes. In fact the next time somebody puts a price on your head, I'd advise you to take it.

Pye All right then, Mr Smarty-pants. How come if I'm so stupid, I happen to know more than you do?

Peas *You* know more than *I* do? (*He laughs*)

Pye (*nodding*) *And* I can prove it.

Peas This I can't wait to see.

Pye Listen. I'll let you ask me a question, and if I can't answer it correctly, I'll give you a pound.

Peas It's money for old rope, dear boy.

Pye Ah—but then I'll ask you a question, and if you can't answer it, you have to pay me two pounds.

Peas (*laughing*) If you can ask me something I don't know, I'll give you *ten* pounds.

Pye Right. Here's my pound. (*He puts it on the floor*)

Peas And here's my ten. (*He puts ten pounds down*)

Pye Now I'll ask the first question. What's got three legs, five wings four wheels and half a jet-engine?

Peas (*baffled*) I've no idea.

Pye laughs and scoops up the money

Just a minute. Just a minute. Before you grab all the cash, what *has* got three legs, five wings, four wheels and half a jet-engine?

Pye I don't know either. Here's your pound.

Pye dashes off laughing

Peas looks at the pound note, reacts, then chases off after Pye

Duke Frederick wearily totters in UR. He is followed by Jack, Jill, two Soldiers, Martha, Tommy, Melody and Colin. All are exhausted and bedraggled, and move along slowly with feet only just clearing the ground

Tommy (*to the audience; weakly*) Hiya, kids. (*He slumps and trudges on*)

Duke It's no use. I can't go on.

The Duke staggers and Jack and Jill catch hold of him

Colin (*calling*) Keep moving, Your Grace. Don't stop.

Duke (*sagging further*) I've got to. I'm finished.

Melody (*desperately*) Uncle Frederick.

Jack and Jill stagger off DL with the Duke and exit. The two Soldiers, Tommy and Melody follow calling anxiously and exit

Colin moves to exit DL *after the others*

  Mother Shipton enters R

Colin (*seeing her*) Mother Shipton. Save us.

  He exits slowly as Mother Shipton calls after him

Mother Shipton Oh Colin, Colin, use the brain that Mother Nature
                              gave you.
                      You need no help to break this spell. Intelligence can
                              save you.
                      The curse was placed on *leathered feet*—so think. No
                              time to lose.
                      To stop this march in safety, simply toss aside your
                              shoes.
(*She gives a sigh of relief and addresses the audience*)
                      Thank goodness I arrived in time to lend a helping hand.
                      But ere Maleficent finds out things haven't gone as
                              planned,
                      We'd best begin our journey to the regions far below;
                      For there to meet his destiny, young Colin now must go.

  Colin, Jack, Melody and Jill hurry in, shoeless

Melody (*embracing Mother Shipton*) Oh, thank you for saving us.
Jill We'd have been turned to stone like all the rest of them if you hadn't
arrived.
Mother Shipton (*smiling*)
  ·   No need for thanks. At least, not yet.
         The danger's still not passed.
         Maleficent will soon be here
         Another spell to cast.

All look dismayed

         But fear you not. Ere she arrives with fury in her heart,
         We'll both be well upon our way. Come Colin, let's depart.
Colin (*bewildered*) But—where are we going? And what about the others?
Jack Yes. You can't just leave us here. We've got nothing to protect
ourselves with.
Mother Shipton Don't worry. She won't bother you when she hears
                              Colin's heading
                      For a certain place inside this hill—and in *my* footsteps
                              treading.
                      His task? To find a casket resting in some rocky bower
                      That holds the key to take away Maleficent's great
                              power.
All react

Colin You mean there's a possibility we can beat her at her own game?

Mother Shipton (*smiling*)
>   Where there's life, there's *always* hope.
>   And though I hate to boast.
>   With *me* to guide your actions
>   You've a better chance than most.
>   So quickly now, your farewells give,
>   No more procrastination.
>   I'll wait for you by yonder rock (*She indicates off* R)
>   Then—to our destination.

Mother Shipton waves her spoon and exits R

Melody Be careful, Colin.

Jack Yes. I'm sure this isn't going to be as simple as it sounds. Perhaps I'd better come with you.

Colin (*shaking his head*) Someone has to stay and look after the others. Don't forget, Baron Snatcher and his men will still be around even if Maleficent comes after *me*.

Jill He's right, Jack. Poor Martha's in no state to protect herself, and neither is the Grand Old Duke. We'd better try and find somewhere to hide them until Colin gets back.

Jack (*uncertain*) Well . . .

Jill Come on. We'll go tell the others what's happening. That'll give Colin and Melody a chance to say their goodbyes in private. (*She pulls at Jack's hand*) Good luck, Colin.

Jack And take care.

Jack and Jill exit DL

Colin Cheer up, Melody. I'll be back before you realize I'm gone. Once that casket's in my hands, we'll have nothing more to worry about. Maleficent will be powerless and Baron Snatcher and his men will be running for their lives.

Melody But what if something goes wrong?

Colin (*laughing*) How can it? With Mother Shipton guiding me, there's not a chance in the world. But . . . (*He hesitates*)

Melody (*anxiously*) But what?

Colin (*wryly*) I wish I didn't have to go barefoot.

Melody (*smiling*) You don't. Look. (*She points to the shoes*) Someone's left a heap of shoes and boots over there.

Colin (*brightening*) What a stroke of luck. (*He crosses to them and selects a pair*) Perfect. (*He slips the shoes on*) And just about my size. (*He moves around to get the feel of them*) Now to find that casket. Before tomorrow morning the Grand Old Duke will be back in power and everything else will be back to normal.

Melody I hope so.

Colin I promise it. And shortly afterwards, the bells of York Minster will be ringing out the news that two of the happiest people in the world are being married.

SONG 10

After the song, Colin cheerily exits R

Martha remains where she is, waving him off

Jack and Jill enter supporting the Grand Old Duke. Martha and Tommy totter in after them

Duke (*groaning*) Ohhhhhhhh, my poor feet. I never want to march another step for as long as I live.

Martha Me neither. Ooooooh, the agony. Those shoes were crippling me.

Tommy I'm not surprised. You were wearing them on the wrong feet.

Martha (*pushing him*) Oh, don't be so stupid. How could I have been wearing them on the wrong feet? These are the only feet I've got.

Melody Speaking of feet. There's quite a pile of shoes here. (*She indicates them*) We'd better try to find ourselves some before we set off back to the City.

Duke Back to the City? Oh, no. It's impossible. I can't walk another step.

The others begin to try on shoes

Jack I'm afraid we have to, Your Grace. We've got to find some place to hide.

Duke Why don't we hide up here? Heaven knows, there's enough stones to shelter us. (*Sadly*) Nearly ten thousand of them. (*He dabs his eyes*)

Jill Oh, don't cry, Your Grace. As soon as Colin gets back with that casket, I'm sure we'll be able to bring them back to life again.

Duke (*brightening*) Do you really think so?

Everyone agrees

Ohhhhhh. (*He sniffles*) I'm feeling better already. (*Fiercely*) But if ever I see that Maleficent woman again, I'll—I'll . . . (*He quivers with fury*)

There is a crash of thunder and Maleficent appears with a green light on her

Maleficent (*triumphantly*) Ahaaaaaaaa! (*She points at them*)

All react in fright

Martha Oh, blimey. It's (*Well-known TV personality*) again.

Maleficent Well, well, well, and deary me: it seems you've found a way
                To break the spell I placed on you. How clever, I *must* say.

Tommy (*preening himself*) Oh, thank you.

Tommy steps back in fright as she glowers at him

Maleficent But all the same, *dear people*, you shan't escape my curse,
                For here and now I'll place on you a spell that's *ten times worse*.

Melody (*defiantly*) Go on, then. Cast your spell. But when Colin finds that casket, you'll be sorry.

Maleficent (*sharply*) Casket? What casket? (*She grabs Melody's arm*) *What* casket?

Duke (*afraid for Melody*) The—the—the one hidden inside this hill—that can take away your powers.

Maleficent (*releasing Melody*) So—you know of the great Talisman, do you?

Jack Of course we do. We've known about it all along.

Maleficent (*smirking*) Have you, my little peacock? But did you also know about its Guardian? The dreadful keeper of the Crystal Cave?

All exchange glances

A thing so hideous that none can look upon it without trembling.

Martha Good heavens. Fancy keeping a photograph of yourself down there.

Jack (*recovering himself*) Well—with Old Mother Shipton helping him, I don't think an ugly, old Guardian is going to be any problem.

Maleficent (*stunned*) Mother *Shipton*?

Jill (*sweetly*) That's right. Do you know her?

Maleficent (*furiously*) That long-nosed Witch from Knaresbro' . . . ?
How *dare* she interfere?
She'll rue the day her path crossed *mine*.
That slip shall cost her dear. (*She snarls*)
Your lives—for now—I'll have to spare.
More urgent is my need
To stop them ere they reach that place
And carry out the deed. (*She gives an evil chuckle*)
By magic arts I'll get there first,
Surprise—then overpow'r them.
Within my web, two flies I'll catch,
And at my ease—*devour them*.

Maleficent swirls around and exits R

The Lights return to normal

Melody (*alarmed*) We've got to warn them. If they walk into her trap they'll be done for.

Jill Yes. And then she'll be back to finish *us* off.

Jack (*grimly*) You're right. We've got to find our way to that cave. Follow me.

Melody, Jack and Jill hurry off R

Martha and Tommy begin to follow, but the Grand Old Duke hangs back

Tommy (*looking over his shoulder*) Come on, or we're going to get left behind.

Duke Oh—er—*I* don't mind. Really, I don't. As a matter of fact I was just thinking—I—er—I'd better stay here and wait till you all get back, anyway. I mean—there doesn't seem to be any need for us *all* to go, does there?

Martha What do you mean, "There doesn't seem to be any need"? Of course there is. We're going to need all the help we can get.

Duke Oh—er—but I thought I could perhaps look after the poor soldiers who escaped with us. They're very upset, you know. They're suffering from shock.

Martha Yes. And I know somebody else who'll be suffering from shock if he doesn't put some shoes on and come with us in *this* direction.

Duke (*face crumpling*) Oh, don't be angry with me, Martha. You know it wouldn't do any good for *me* to come with you. I'm just a cowardly old man—and I'm *scared*. (*He cries*)

Tommy (*amazed*) Well, I'll go to the foot of our stairs. And *I* thought they had problems in (*TV soap opera*). Listen, Your Washup, *I'm* scared. *Martha's* scared. Everybody's scared.

Duke (*still sobbing*) Yes, but you're not half as scared as me. I'd be no use at all if there were any trouble.

Martha (*indicating Tommy*) And what use do you think *he'd* be? He's about as much use as a brain is to an Irishman.

Tommy (*indignantly*) Here—less of the Irish jokes if you don't mind. My father was Irish, and there was nothing wrong with *his* brain.

Martha Listen, shillelagh features ... Your father was so stupid, he thought Sherlock Holmes was a *block of flats*. And what did he do when he won those water skis in the Christmas Raffle last Easter? He spent the next six months trying to find a lake that *sloped*. (*To the Duke*) Now then, let's get *you* sorted out. So you're scared, are you? Frightened of your own shadow? Well then, why don't you do what *we* do?

Duke What's that?

Martha We *whistle*.

Duke Whistle?

Tommy Whistle.

Duke But what good does that do?

Martha Come on, Tommy. Let's tell him.

SONG 11

Tommy and Martha sing and the Duke and audience provide a whistling accompaniment

At the end of the song, Martha, Tommy and the Duke dance off R *cheerily. As they do so, the Baron, Pye and Peas enter* L

Baron (*smirking*) What a good thing we happened to be close by and overheard everything. Now's our chance to get rid of them once and for all. Quickly. After them. With Maleficent in front and us behind, we've got them *trapped*. (*He laughs in triumph*)

The three set off in pursuit

Black-out

SCENE 2

A Rocky Gorge. Evening

The Babes, dressed as Pixies, enter carrying lanterns made to look like flower heads. The Juniors may also join in if required

A short dance to music is performed

  After the routine all exit quickly

  Colin and Mother Shipton enter R

Mother Shipton The secret entrance lies just there (*She points off* L)
                             Behind that mighty boulder.
                             A simple push will clear the way,
                             So quick. Apply your shoulder.
Colin No sooner said than done.

  He exits L

Mother Shipton (*to the audience*)
    So far, so good. For up to now we've kept one jump ahead.
    But from here on, we'll have to watch *exactly* how we tread.
    One slight mistake on Colin's part, and all, I fear, is lost.
    So wish him luck, please, boys and girls,
    And keep your fingers crossed.

  Colin enters brushing his hands

Colin Well that's taken care of that—but what are we going to do about
a light? It looks awfully dark in there.
Mother Shipton No matter. There'll be light enough to find the thing
                             you seek;
                             But one more item's needed ere you venture 'neath this
                             peak. (*She signals off* R)

  Two Pixies enter carrying a gleaming sword on a long, velvet cushion

                             Behold. The Sword of Chivalry, Defender of Just Cause.
                             With this, all wrongs are put to right. Come take it. It
                             is yours.

  In awe, Colin takes the sword

                             Success now rests within your grasp, so to that cavern
                             grim
                             Wherein the fearsome Guardian dwells. It's time to
                             meet with *him*.

  *With a flourish of her wooden spoon Mother Shipton crosses in front of
  Colin and exits* L. *Colin follows her*

  The Two Pixies wave to them as the Lights fade to a Black-out

SCENE 3

A Great Cavern inside the Enchanted Hill

There are several exits R *and* L *representing caves. Glittering stalagmites and
stalactites form the backdrop and sides. There is a large rock upstage just off*

CR, *and a smaller one* (*which serves as a seat*) *in front of it. A gaping passage-way is situated* L *of the rocks, lit from within in red, green and blue. If space will not permit this make* UL *an exit point*

The Lights come up on a host of Trolls, Goblins and/or Spirits who are engaged in a lively dance. Maleficent is hidden from view behind the large rock

Colin and Mother Shipton enter R *when the music has finished*

The Creatures at once menace them. Colin steps back, but Mother Shipton remains calm

Mother Shipton Fear not. Your magic sword from any harm will keep
           us free.
           Just show them you mean business and their backs
             you'll *quickly* see.

Colin raises his sword and the Creatures retreat with loud hisses and wails

   The Creatures exit in all directions

           Now hurry. Time is getting short. Search ev'ry inch of
             ground.
           If you seek here, I'll check in there.
(*She indicates the tunnel*)
           That casket *must* be found.

   Mother Shipton exits into the tunnel

Colin (*gazing around*) I never dreamed the place would be so huge. It's going to take ages to search through all these caves. (*He goes and peers into a cave-entrance and then shrugs*) Well, there's certainly nothing hidden in there. I'd better try the next one along.

He begins to move L, *sword at the ready. As he is about to exit, the anxious calls of Melody, Jack and Jill from off* R *cause him to turn in surprise*

Melody ⎱
Jack   ⎬ (*together, off*) ⎰ Colin, Mother Shipton. Where are you?
Jill   ⎰
Colin (*calling*) Over here. This way.

   Melody, Jack and Jill enter breathlessly

Melody Oh, Colin. Thank goodness we managed to find you in time.
Jill We just *had* to come and warn you.
Jack Maleficent's set a trap for you. She's hiding somewhere inside these caves.
Colin (*glancing quickly around*) Is she, indeed? Then the sooner we find that casket, the better.
Melody Where's Mother Shipton?

Colin (*pointing*) She went to look through there. I'd better go warn her.

Jack Right. And while you're doing that, Jill and I will search through that cave over there. (*He indicates* DR)

Colin (*nodding*) But don't go too far alone. Remember, there's still the Guardian of the Cave to watch out for.

Jill Don't worry. If I see him first, I'll scream the place down. (*To Jack*) Come on.

Jack and Jill hurry off DR *and Colin and Melody hurry off into the tunnel*

A huge spider drops from the roof of the cavern and vanishes behind a rock
A moment later Maleficent appears from behind the rock, chuckling

Maleficent Seek on, you fools. The box you seek was found by little *me*.
           I've got it tucked behind that rock as safe as safe can be.
           Now by my magic pow'rs I'll cause the Guardian to appear
           And finish off the *lot* of you, whilst I get out of here.
(*She raises her wand to cast a spell, then gives a yelp of pain and clutches her shoulder tightly*)
           Ooooooh. (*Annoyed*) A plague on stupid caves like these
           Devoid of central heating.
           Of all the places I *dislike*, this *really* takes some beating.
(*Full of self-pity*)
           The draught affects me rheumatiz, the damp, me bronchial
              chest.
           The cold brings on me chilblains (and that's something I
              detest.)
           I've spots before me eyeballs, so it's hard for me to see.
           And an *agonizing* pain around me arthritic knee.
           There's a swelling like a gumboil just behind an aching tooth,
           And me floating kidney's *sinking* . . . It's the pure and
              honest truth.
           Me sinuses are stuffed up and there's wax inside me ear . . .
           It's no wonder I'm bad-tempered when I have to work down
              here. (*She shrugs philosophically*)
           Oh, well, it's no use grumbling, for no-one cares a hang.
           The Guardian I'll summon *now*, to finish off that gang.
(*She raises her wand cautiously*)
           By magic spell I summon you from deep inside your lair.
           Come, mighty Guardian of the Caves . . .

Martha (*off*) Is anybody there?

Maleficent (*whirling around in annoyance*) Curses. *Tourists!*

Tommy (*off*) Yoo-hoo. Colin. Mother Shipyard?

Maleficent So . . . Once again I'll have to hide in order to surprise.
           I'll go behind the rock and there assume my spider guise.
(*She hurries behind the rock*)
The spider shoots upwards to the roof a moment ater

Tommy and Martha (*who is carrying a picnic basket*) *enter*

Tommy (*to the audience*) Hiya, kids. (*He looks round*) Oooh. Innit eerie? It's just like the inside of a Mecca Ballroom.

Martha suddenly lets out a loud shriek

Whazzermarrer? Wharizzit? What's wrong?
Martha (*frozen*) Don't move. Don't take another step.

Tommy freezes. Martha sniffs the air several times

(*Almost in a whisper*) I can *smell* it.
Tommy (*in a whisper*) Smell what?
Martha (*in a whisper*) *IT*.

Tommy looks blank, then timorously sniffs the air too. Detecting nothing unusual, he gives a quick glance at the soles of his shoes

I'd know that smell anywhere. It's here. Inside this very cave.
Tommy (*uneasily*) Oh—well . . . (*He glances around fearfully*) We'd better try not to tread in it, then, hadn't we?
Martha (*impatiently pushing him*) Not *that*, fat-head. I'm talking about *spiders*. Inside this cave is a *spider*.
Tommy (*relaxing*) Oh, come on Martha. Of course there isn't a spider down here.
Martha Oh, yes there is.
Tommy Oh, no there isn't. How could a spider get down here?
Martha I don't know and I don't care, but there's one lurking somewhere down here or my name isn't Martha Muffett. (*She gives a knowing laugh*) I know all about spiders, I do. I'm a woman with experience.
Tommy So everybody keeps telling me. Anyway, never mind about spiders. We came down here to look for Colin and the others, so let's get on with it. (*He moves away from her*)
Martha Just a minute. Just a minute. I'm not moving anywhere until somebody gets rid of that spider. (*She puts down her basket*)
Tommy (*shrugging*) All right, then. You'll have to stay there till I get back. But don't forget. The longer you stay there, the more chance there is of the Guardian of the Cave catching you.
Martha Eh? (*She blinks*)
Tommy (*nodding*) In case you'd forgotten, you're standing right in the middle of his living-room.
Martha (*nervously*) *I am?* (*She looks round*) Oooooh! I don't think much to his wallpaper. (*She moves quickly towards Tommy*) Perhaps I'd better come with you, after all. You—er—you might need a bit of protection.
Tommy *I* might need protection?
Martha Yes, you're right. But don't you worry. Martha's with you. (*Suddenly*) Here—I've just thought on. What's happened to the Grand Old Duke? Where is he? (*She looks round*)
Tommy Oh, don't worry about *him*. He's waiting for us near the entrance.
Martha (*shrewdly*) *How* near the entrance?
Tommy (*indicating with thumb and finger a small gap*) About a mile.
Martha (*tiredly*) I don't know why I bothered asking. I might have guessed.

One sniff of trouble, and he's off like a rocket. He spends so much time chewing his nails, his stomach needs a manicure. (*Brightening*) Still, it's an ill wind that gathers no moss, isn't it? (*She beams at Tommy*)

Tommy (*startled*) Eh?

Martha I mean . . . If he's not *with* us, you know what *that* means, don't you?

Tommy No.

Martha (*coyly*) It means we're *alone*. By ourselves. Together. Just you and me.

Tommy (*with foreboding*) W-what about it?

Martha Well, here we are—with nobody to disturb us . . . So now's our chance to put a little romance into our lives. Come on. Give us a kiss. (*She puckers up her lips*)

Tommy (*retreating*) Er—er—er—er . . . Wait. I mean—why do you want me to kiss you *now*? Can't we wait till after we've found the others?

Martha (*firmly*) No, we can't. We're engaged to be bridalized, and I want my rights. Now come on. Plant one on these. (*She puckers her lips*)

Tommy (*squirming*) Oh, Martha, don't you think we're a bit too *old* for that sort of thing?

Martha Old? *Old*? (*Grimly*) Listen, jug-ears. *You* might be too old, but *I'm* still in the first flush of youth.

Tommy Oh, give over. There were so many candles on your last birthday cake, it looked like a torchlight procession.

Martha Really? (*Her lips tighten in annoyance*)

Tommy Anyway. I can't kiss you now. I'm too hungry. I haven't eaten a thing since yesterday morning, and I'm starving.

Martha (*brightening*) Well, why didn't you say so? I've got just the very thing. (*She gets her basket*) Curds and whey sandwiches. (*She opens the basket*)

Tommy Curds and whey *sandwiches*?

Martha Yes. They're smashing. Come on. We'll sit on that rock and eat 'em.

They move to the rock and sit. Martha hands out the sandwiches, placing the basket near her feet. As they eat, the spider drops to above their heads. On the audience reaction, both look startled

Tommy (*nervously*) What is it? What are they shouting for?

Martha (*clutching at him*) It's that spider. The one I told you about. It's after me curds and whey sandwiches. (*She looks around worriedly*)

Tommy (*gulping*) I can't see any spiders. (*He looks around*)

Martha Neither can I—but *they* can. Come on. Lets have a look for it.

they get up to look round and the spider shoots up and vanishes

Well, there doesn't seem to be any spider round here.

Tommy No—but I'll tell you what. I'll ask my mates out there to give us a yell if they see it again. (*To the audience*) Will you do that, kids? Just shout out and tell us if you see the spider trying to pinch our sandwiches. Thanks a lot.

They go back to the rock and sit. As they start to eat, the spider drops again and they ad-lib with the audience for a few moments

(*To Martha*) Oh, they're having us on. They know you're scared of spiders and they're just trying to frighten you.

Martha Yes. You're right. Well the next time they shout out, we'll take no notice of 'em.

They begin to eat again. The spider drops to just above them. Tommy looks up and sees it. He springs to his feet with a yell. Martha looks up and sees it. Quickly, she gets a large mallet from her basket and hits the spider with it. It falls behind the rock

Wonder Woman strikes again. (*She waves the mallet*)

Tommy (*moving to peer behind the rock*) Coo—you haven't half given it a lump on the head. Hey—and *look*.

He goes behind the rock and comes out with a small casket

Martha What is it? (*She drops the mallet and hurries to see*)

Tommy It's a little box. And there's something inside it.

Martha (*eagerly*) Perhaps it's the one Colin's looking for. Quick. Open it up.

As they struggle to open the lid, Maleficent staggers out from behind the rock, clutching her head

Maleficent (*groaning*) Oooooooooooooh!

Tommy and Martha turn to see her

Tommy Oh, heck. It's her again.

Maleficent (*furiously*) For that attack, revenge I'll take.
　　　　　　　　You both shall die, I vow.
　　　　　　　　(*Loudly*) Come mighty Guardian of the Caves . . .
　　　　　　　　I call you here and now. (*She waves her wand*)

The Guardian appears in a great flash of lightning and with a loud roar. Martha and Tommy stagger back in fright

Martha It's Arthur Scargill (*or well-known politician, etc.*)

Maleficent (*pointing to Tommy and Martha*) Destroy them!

The Guardian advances on them and they yell with fright

Jack and Jill run in DR, *and Colin, Melody and Mother Shipton enter from the tunnel. All react*

Colin (*to the others*) Stand back. I'll deal with him.

Colin springs in front of the Guardian, sword poised. Maleficent scuttles back DL *and the others cower* R. *A fierce battle takes place and eventually Colin kills the Guardian. All react*

(*Turning to Maleficent*) And now to deal with you.

Maleficent You stupid boy, discard your sword. Its powers can't match *mine*.

Mother Shipton (*stepping forward*) But *those* pow'rs can, my fairy friend
If we should so incline. (*She indicates the casket
Martha holds*)

Everyone looks at the casket

Maleficent (*unable to believe her eyes*) The Talisman. They found it.

Mother Shipton takes the casket

Mother Shipton The game is up, Maleficent; you'd best admit defeat.
We've got the upper hand at last. You're well and
truly *beat*.

Maleficent I won't be beaten. I won't.

Mother Shipton opens the casket and takes out the Talisman

Mother Shipton By virtue of this Talisman, I take away your powers.

*Mother Shipton holds up the Talisman and a beam of white light falls on to
Maleficent who gives a loud wail*

Now go. Your magic is no more and victory is ours.

Maleficent covers her face and still moaning exits L. *The white spot goes
out. All congratulate each other*

Colin (*handing his sword to Jack*) And now to return to York and put
everything back to normal. With this in our hands—(*he indicates the
Talisman*)—we can bring all the Grand Duke's men back to life *and*
rebuild the City walls.

Jack Not to mention, get rid of Baron Snatcher.

Melody We must find Uncle Frederick at once and tell him the good news.

Mother Shipton One moment. Ere you dash away to spread your
greetings glad.
There's more adventure yet for you and this young
Gypsy lad.

Jill *More* adventure?

Colin (*puzzled*) I don't understand. What can possibly happen to us now?
So long as we have the Talisman to protect us, we should be safe
forever.

Mother Shipton Quite so. And yet despite your hopes, you're going to
come to grief.
That Talisman, I vow, will soon be stolen by a common
thief.

Martha Over Tommy's dead body. The first person to lay hands on that
Talisman without my permission is going to have me to reckon with.
Here. (*She holds out the box*) Put it back in this for safety.

Colin puts the Talisman back in the casket

(*Handing it to Tommy*) Now you hold on to this and guard it with your
life.

Tommy Don't worry, Martha. If anybody tries to pinch this, they'll have to take me with it.

Martha Well if *that* doesn't put 'em off, nothing will. Now come on everybody. Back to York.

Before they can move, the Baron's Guards rush in, swords drawn. The Baron, Pye and Peas, also armed, follow

Melody (*alarmed*) Look out!

Colin Quick. The Talisman. (*He makes a grab for the casket*)

Baron Too late. (*He snatches it out of Tommy's hands*) The Talisman is mine. (*To the Guards*) Seize them.

The Guards quickly disarm Jack and capture the others

(*Sneering*) So . . . You thought to outwit me, did you? Steal my title and hand the City back to that pathetic old idiot, Frederick? How fortunate I managed to follow you here and discover what you were up to. (*He glances around*) But where is the dear Grand Duke? He doesn't seem to be here.

Pye Don't you worry about him, boss. We'll soon find him, won't we, Peas? (*He waves his sword*)

Peas Oh, undoubtedly. Ten minutes and we'll have him trussed up like a Christmas turkey. (*He smirks*)

Baron Bah. You two idiots couldn't find a lost weekend, never mind the Grand Duke. I'll deal with him myself as soon as we get this lot back to my castle. (*To the Guards*) To my dungeons with 'em.

The Guards begin prodding the Prisoners

Colin (*grimly*) You won't get away with this.

Baron Silence, you snivelling Gypsy brat. With this Talisman in my hands I can get away with *anything*. One more word from you, and you'll find yourself turned into a lump of rock just like all those other fools who followed the Grand Old Duke.

Mother Shipton (*sharply*) You'll live to rue the day you mocked
　　　　　　　　　Those stones with foolish talk.
　　　　　　　　　I hereby vow they'll *rise again*
　　　　　　　　　To keep in safety ancient York.

Baron (*with a snort of amusement*) Will they? Well there's one thing certain—*you* won't be around to see it happen. By this time tomorrow you'll be burning at the stake. We want no witches in York. (*To the Guards*) Away with them.

The Prisoners are pushed out of the cavern by the Guards as Baron Snatcher roars with laughter and holds up the casket

The Lights fade to a Black-out

SCENE 4

A Quiet Path on the Hillside

The Guards enter L *escorting the prisoners Colin, Melody, Jack, Jill, Martha and Tommy. Pye, Peas and the Baron follow them on*

Tommy (*to the audience*) Hiya, kids.

A Guard prods Tommy with his sword and he yells

They all cross R *and exit as Duke Frederick enters cautiously* L *at the same time. He scurries* R *and gazes off after them*

Duke (*anguished*) Oh dear. That nasty old Baron's captured everybody *and* got hold of the Talisman. Whatever are we going to do now? I've just *got* to help them escape—but how? (*He plunges into deep thought, chewing at his fingernails*)

Maleficent enters L *in black despair*

Maleficent Whoever thought I'd end like this—robbed of me magic
              powers?
              I've simply *got* to get them back. But *how*? I've thought for
                  hours.
              I'll have to plead with Frederick and beg on bended knees,
              Promise that I'll change me ways and always try to please.
              Say good-bye to wicked plots and be as nice as pie,
              If in return he'll give to me my powers, by and by.
                  (*Annoyed*)
              Ten thousand curses. How I hate to just throw in the sponge.
              For two pins I'd . . . (*She sees the Duke*) Duke Frederick . . .
                  (*She shrugs*)
              Oh, well, I'll take the plunge. (*She crosses to him and taps him
                  on the shoulder*)

Duke (*surprised*) Huh? (*He turns and sees her*) Aaaaaaaagh! (*He backs away*)

Maleficent (*falling to one knee with head bowed*) O mighty Duke. I kneel to you.

Duke (*petrified with fright*) Heeeeeelp. (*He realizes*) Pardon?

Maleficent Forgive me for all my nasty deeds and I promise you I'll never be wicked again.

Duke (*unsure of what he is hearing*) You will? (*He blinks*) Ooooh, wait a minute. Wait a minute. This is just a trick, isn't it? You're making fun of me.

Maleficent No, no. I know when I'm beaten. Just tell me that you'll forgive me and I'll be your slave for life.

Duke (*uncertainly*) Oh—well . . . (*To the audience*) Do *you* think I should forgive her, boys and girls? (*He waits for audience reaction*) Well, I don't think they're too happy about the idea, Miss Maleficent.

Maleficent grovels

Oh—all right. I forgive you . . . But only on one condition.

Maleficent Name it. Anything at all.

Duke You've got to help me put everything back to normal again.

Maleficent (*eagerly*) Yes, yes. Of course.

Duke (*lifting her gently*) Now *do* get up. This damp grass must be playing havoc with your rheumatism.

Maleficent Yes, yes. I *do* get nasty twinges in conditions like this.

Duke (*nodding*) I know. I get it round the elbow. And the shoulders.

Maleficent The back of my neck's the worst.

They compare locations for a few moments

Duke (*brisky*) Oh, well, back to business. Now then . . . First of all, we've got to get into that castle you built for Baron Snatcher—and without anyone seeing us.

Maleficent Very well. Give me the Talisman and I'll show you how we do it.

Duke (*blankly*) Talisman? Oh—I can't do *that*. You see . . .

Maleficent (*interrupting*) Yes, I know. You still don't entirely trust me, is that it?

Duke No, no. Not at all. We're *friends* now. Of course I trust you. No—the truth of the matter is . . .

Maleficent (*interrupting again*) No matter. No matter. We don't have to use the Talisman if you'd rather not. We can go through the secret passage that leads to the castle dungeons.

Duke (*delighted*) We can?

Maleficent Oh, yes. I always put a secret passage in my magic castles—just in case of emergencies. (*She chuckles*)

Duke How sensible of you, my dear Maleficent. Now quickly. Take me to it.

Maleficent No need, dear Frederick. It's right behind you. (*She points off*) At the back of yonder rock.

Duke (*excitedly*) Come on, then. Once inside the castle you can use your magic powers to rescue everybody from the Baron, and then we can have a go at getting the Talisman back from him.

Maleficent (*stunned*) Baron Snatcher has the Talisman? (*Fuming*) Do you mean to tell me that *Baron Snatcher has the Talisman?*

Duke (*puzzled at the change in attitude*) Well—yes. He stole it from us and captured all my . . .

Maleficent (*outraged*) How *dare* you make me look a fool and grovel
             at your feet.
             Revenge, I swear, I'll have for this. Revenge that's
             swift and sweet.
             Within the hour a spell I'll cast to make you
             shriek with fear.
             You'll be condemned to spend your holidays at
             Butlins ev'ry year.

Maleficent whirls round and exits L, *fuming*

Duke (*calling*) Wait. Wait, I thought we were going to be friends? (*Dejectedly*) Honestly. She changes sides more often than a windscreen-wiper. (*Worried*) Now it looks as though I'll have to rescue them all on my own. Oh dear. Still, it's a good job she told me how to get into the castle. I'd better hurry before she warns them I'm coming.

He exits R

Black-out

Scene 5

The Throneroom of the Black Castle

A large room with a huge throne R. *Guards stand at each side of the room Baron Snatcher, the Talisman round his neck, is sitting in splendour wearing an ermine-edged robe and the Crown of York. Pye and Peas sit at his feet. As the Lights come up several couples are performing a stately gavotte to music, but though dressed in attractive costumes, all have the faces of animals*

When the dance ends, all bow low to the Baron who waves them aside. They move back against the walls of the room as he rises

Baron (*sneering*) Yes, you do well to bow to me, you scurvy knaves. By the power of this magic Talisman I've turned you all into monsters, and monsters you'll stay until I decide otherwise. (*To Pye and Peas*) Now where are the prisoners I captured this morning?
Pye (*jumping up*) We'll get 'em for you boss. We've got 'em all locked in the dungeons.

Peas begins to rise as the Baron turns to face them

Baron Boss? *Boss?* (*Fiercely*) Now that I'm Grand Duke of York, you don't call me "boss". If you wish to speak to me, you address me *properly*. Understand?
Pye (*nodding furiously*) Yes, boss.
Baron (*preens himself*) You must first say "Your Grace".
Peas Ah, yes. (*He recites*) For what we are about to receive . . .
Baron (*very annoyed*) *No*, you blockhead. (*He groans*) Oh, go get the prisoners and be quick about it. I want to *gloat* over them. (*He leers*)
Pye We'll have 'em here before you can say Jack Robinson.
Baron (*snarling*) You'd better, because if you don't, I'll turn your heads into turnips and *boil them*, Now move.

Pye and Peas look terrified and scuttle off L

(*Chuckling*) Oho, what a nasty piece of knitting I really am. With this Talisman in my hands, I can rule the *Universe*. My slightest wish will be obeyed. Nothing, absolutely nothing, shall be denied me. (*He smirks*) I might even put an end to "Crossroads". (*He leers at the audience*)

Maleficent scuttles in L

Maleficent He he he he he.

The Baron spins round, startled

How now, Grand Duke? (*She gives him an exaggerated curtsy*)

Baron (*snarling*) What are you doing here, you old crone?

Maleficent (*taken aback*) Why, I come to celebrate our victory, of course.

Baron *Our* victory? (*Nastily*) You mean *my* victory, don't you? I seem to remember that old witch, Mother Shipton, turning the tables on *you* and taking away your magic powers.

Maleficent (*waving it aside*) A pure accident. But now we have the Talisman back again, I can soon recover them. Give it to me. (*She reaches*)

Baron (*snarling*) Not so fast, you bottle-nosed old bat. This Talisman belongs to *me*. You're not getting your grasping little mitts on it—not even for a second.

Maleficent But my powers . . .

Baron (*leering*) *That* for your powers. (*He tries to snap his fingers, but fails*) I'm not having you tottering round my City casting spells anywhere you like. *I'm* in charge from now on, and the only one doing magic is me. Now clear off before I do something I'd *enjoy* doing.

Maleficent (*seething*) So be it. Once again I'm made to look an utter fool.

From henceforth "Trust no mortal" shall be *my* Golden Rule.

But ere I leave, remember this—"Pride goes before a fall";

And yours, I vow, Grand Duke of York, will be the greatest fall of all.

Maleficent swirls around and exits L in a fury

Baron (*calling*) You don't scare me, you moth-eaten old monstrosity. Without your magic powers, you're done for. (*He laughs harshly and then looks in contempt at the dancers*) And you can clear off too. Go on. move.

The dancers quickly exit

Now where are those prisoners?

Pye enters L

Pye Here they are, boss—I mean Gracie.

The Baron glares at Pye

Colin, Melody, Jack, Jill, Martha, Mother Shipton and Tommy enter followed by Peas and two armed Guards

Tommy (*to the audience*) Hiya, kids. (*Audience response*)

Peas Kneel, dogs. Kneel to His Grace the Grand Duke of York.

Martha You won't get *me* kneeling to that crooked old curmudgeon. He's no grace—he's a dis-grace.

Baron Silence, you old harridan. One more word from you, and I'll give you the head of an ass.

Martha Oh? And what will you do with your crown, then? Balance it on your shoulders?

The Baron gives a snarl of rage and holds up the Talisman to cast a spell. All react

Melody (*quickly*) Oh, no. Please. Don't harm her. I promise you she'll be quiet. (*She motions to Martha to keep silent*)
Baron (*leering at Melody*) Well ... (*He lowers the Talisman*) As you ask so nicely, how can I refuse? (*To Martha*) But remember—one more word ...

The Baron turns his back on Martha to go to the throne. As he does so, she quickly sticks her tongue out

Colin (*boldly*) Well? I suppose we were brought here for *some* reason. Do you intend telling us what it is?
Baron (*spinning round to face him*) Silence when you speak to me, Gypsy boy. (*He glares*) I'll tell you in my own good time. (*He smiles*) But first of all I want to hear you pleading for mercy. (*He sits*)
Colin (*amused*) That'll be the day.
Baron (*annoyed*) Will it? You'll change your tune when I have you dangling from the gallows in my courtyard.

All react

Colin I wouldn't count on it. But there is *one* thing you could do. Let the others go free and show them that you *do* have a heart.

The Baron roars with laughter

I thought it wouldn't be much use asking you to behave like an ordinary, decent human being.
Tommy You're right. He doesn't do impersonations. (*He chortles*)
Baron (*standing in a fury*) One more interruption and I'll have the lot of you flogged—except that charming little creature over there. (*He leers at Melody*) I've got other plans for *her*. (*To Melody*) Tell me, my dear, wouldn't you like to share this throne with me? To be my *bride*.
Melody (*with a shudder*) I'd rather die.
Martha (*to the Baron*) And it's no use looking at me, either. *I* wouldn't marry you if you were the last man on earth. Mind you, it could have its advantages. I could teach you how to play "puss in the corner".
Baron "Puss in the corner"?
Martha Yes. *You* stand in the corner, and *I* kick you in the puss.
Baron (*roaring*) Silence, you brainless old bat.
Tommy Temper, temper. There's children watching out there, you know. (*He indicates the audience*) You have to set them an example.
Baron (*fuming*) I'll set them an example, all right. Guards, take these idiots back to the dungeons and give them all five hundred lashes.
Martha Blimey. I've heard of a whip-round, but that's ridiculous.

The Guards, Pye and Peas menace the Prisoners

Baron (*indicating Melody*) Not that one. She stays with me. (*He grabs her by the arm*)

Melody (*struggling*) Colin!

Colin (*trying to reach her*) Let go of her! Let go!

The Baron laughs as Colin is driven back

Mother Shipton Don't worry. She won't come to harm, and neither will your friends.
His time of power is running out and very shortly ends.
I see an end to treachery: foretell a future bright.
The Grand Old Duke returns to claim the throne of York tonight.

The Baron laughs

Jack You can laugh, but you'll laugh on the other side of your face when he gets here. He'll find some way of getting inside this place.

Jill Yes. Mother Shipton is *never* wrong.

Baron Is that so? (*He smirks*) Then I'd better take precautions, hadn't I? (*He raises the Talisman*) By the power of this Talisman, I command that should Duke Frederick even dare to set foot in the courtyard, he will die the most horrible death the world has ever known. (*He lowers the Talisman*) *Now* let him try to claim his throne back. (*He laughs*) Away with them.

The Guards, Pye and Peas, drive everyone out, leaving Melody alone with the Baron

And now, my dear. Let's talk about my plans for the future. (*He releases her*)

Melody (*turning her back on him*) Don't even speak to me, you horrible monster.

Baron (*smirking*) You won't call me that when we're married.

Melody I'll never marry you.

Baron Oh, I think you will. If not of your own free will, then with the aid of the Talisman. But consider, as I am now about to become Emperor of the Universe, you could be my Empress, and it's far better to be a live Empress than the darling of a dead thief.

Melody (*turning to him; angrily*) He's not a thief.

Baron All Gypsies are thieves—and so are the people who *mix* with them. But enough. Do I announce our wedding with your consent or not?

Melody Not in a million years.

Baron (*casually*) Not even if I changed my mind about hanging your precious Gypsy boy and his friends?

Melody You mean—you'd let them go free? Without harming them?

Baron Of course. *And* lift the spell on the Grand Old Duke.

Melody (*suspiciously*) I don't believe you.

Baron Do I look like the kind of man who'd tell a lie? (*He tries to look innocent*)

Melody (*uncertainly*) I—I'll have to think about it.

Baron Think away, my precious little jewel. You have all the time in the world. But remember, the quicker you decide, the better it will be for everyone. I'll wait next door for your answer.

The Baron exits R

Melody (*despairingly*) What am I going to do? I can't marry that terrible man, but how else am I to save the others? Wait . . . If I do agree to marry him, it will give Colin another chance to defeat him. And if what Mother Shipton says is true, we're bound to win this time. I'll do it. (*She sings*)

SONG 12

At the end of the song, Melody calls for the Baron, who enters eagerly

Baron Well?

Melody I—I've decided to do as you wish. Lift the spell on Uncle Frederick and free the others, and I'll marry you whenever you like.

Baron (*triumphantly*) I knew you'd see sense. Not only have you the prettiest face I've seen since I looked in the mirror this morning, you have brains too. A perfect combination for the bride of an Emperor. Very well, then. We'll be married at once.

Melody (*startled*) What?

Baron (*leering at her*) I'd hate you to change your mind as soon as I'd kept my half of the bargain.

Melody turns away from him

(*Shouting*) Pye! Peas! Where are you, you mutton-headed morons?

Pye and Peas come hurrying in

Cancel the whippings and prepare to release the prisoners.

Pye (*surprised*) Eh?

Peas You mean—you're going to let them go?

Baron I do—but not just yet. They are to be guarded until the pretty Miss Melody and I are married, and after that, *I never want to see them again*. Do you understand? (*He winks*)

Peas (*nodding*) Leave it to us, Your Grace.

Baron (*to Melody*) Now come, my precious one. We must announce our betrothal to the Citizens of York.

Melody is escorted out by the Baron

Pye Here—what did he mean, he never wanted to see them again? Does that mean we've got to banish 'em?

Peas Of course not, you dim-witted dope. The minute he's married to Melody, we've to kill the lot of 'em. Now come on. To the dungeons.

Pye and Peas exit

Black-out

SCENE 6

The Dungeons of the Black Castle

The Lights come up to show a backcloth depicting a dungeon

Colin, Martha, Jack, Jill, Mother Shipton and Tommy are pushed on by the two armed Guards. The Guards then exit

Tommy (*to the audience*) Hiya, kids.

Colin (*to Mother Shipton*) Are you sure things are going to turn out all right, and nothing will happen to Melody?

Mother Shipton (*beaming*) I haven't let you down as yet, I'm sure you all agree.
Duke Frederick is on our track, and shortly we'll be free.

Jack But I don't see how we can be. You heard the spell that Baron Snatcher placed on him.

Jill If he even tries to approach the castle walls, he's doomed to die.

Mother Shipton (*laughing*) The Baron cast his spell too late to do much good, I fear.
Some minutes ere he spoke those words, the Grand Old Duke had *entered* here.

Tommy You mean—he's inside the castle *now*?

Martha Then where *is* he?

Mother Shipton smiles and points R. They all turn to look

Duke Frederick enters R on tip-toe and walking backwards. He carries a rusty old sword

Colin (*delighted*) Your Grace.

Frederick gives a great yell of fright, drops his sword and falls to his knees, covering his eyes

Duke Don't kill me. Don't kill me. I give up. Surrender.

Jill (*running to him*) Duke Frederick. It's us.

Duke (*looking up*) Eh? Oh. (*He recognizes them*) Ohhhhh, thank goodness I've found you. (*He scrambles to his feet*) I've been wandering round this horrible place for ages.

Colin But how did you manage to get here?

Duke Through the secret passageway, but never mind about *that*. I've got the most *dreadful* news to tell you.

Tommy (*glumly*) Don't say (*local football team*) have lost again.

Duke No, no, no, no, no. It's poor Melody. That scoundrel Baron Snatcher is going to marry her. Down in the City Square. I overheard it all. She's agreed to do it to save your lives.

Colin (*aghast*) What?

Martha Ohhhh! That's a fate worse than bad breath.

Jack We've got to stop her, Colin.

Colin But how? We haven't a chance so long as he holds that Talisman.

Jill Then we'll have to get it from him, won't we?

Colin Easier said than done; but all the same, we're not going to achieve much just standing here. (*To the Duke*) Quick, Your Grace. Take us to this secret tunnel. We've got to get to the City Square before they do. We can think of a plan as we go.

Duke Right. Follow me. (*He hesitates*) Er—you go first. (*He indicates* R)

Colin hurries off followed by Jack, Jill and Mother Shipton. The Duke picks up his sword and scurries after them

Tommy is about to follow when he is grabbed by Martha

Martha Not so fast, wanderlust. *We're* not leaving this place until we get one or two things settled.

Tommy Eh? What sort of things?

Martha Well, as this looks like things are coming to a head and old Snatcher's going to get what's coming to him, I want to know how long it's going to be before we start thinking about being bridalized.

Tommy Bridalized?

Martha Yes. When am I going to be your awful wedded wife?

Tommy (*groaning*) Oh, Martha. Don't say you're starting all *that* again?

Martha I certainly am. And don't give me that old excuse about not having any money, because there's bound to be a reward for helping old Freddie to get his crown and things back, so you can use some of your share to smother me with fur coats and jewels.

Tommy (*muttering*) I could do it cheaper with a cushion.

Martha (*sharply*) What was that?

Tommy (*with a sickly grin*) Only joking. All right. Tell me what you want, and as soon as I get the money, I'll buy it for you.

Martha (*delighted*) You will? Well then . . . let me think. (*She thinks*) Oh— I can't make me mind up. I'll leave it up to you. Anything'll do as long as it's got lots and lots of diamonds in it.

Tommy (*stunned*) Diamonds? (*He brightens*) O.K. I'll buy you a deck of playing-cards.

Martha (*annoyed*) Right. That's done it. I'm fed up with you trifling with my emulsions. You can have your cheap little ring back and I'll marry somebody else.

Tommy Here—less of the cheap. That engagement ring once belonged to a multi-millionaire.

Martha Yes. Woolworth.

Tommy Oh, come on. Martha. You wouldn't *really* marry somebody else, would you?

Martha I certainly would. You're not the only feller in York who's noticed how glamorous I am. Only last week a perfect stranger told me that when he looked at me, time stood still.

Tommy Yes. But he meant that your face had stopped his pocket-watch.

Martha (*bawling*) Awwwwwwww!

Tommy Oh, don't cry, Martha. I was only pulling your leg. You know you're the only girl for me.

Martha Am I? (*She sniffles*)
Tommy Course you are.
Martha Well . . . what is it about me you like most? Is it my looks?
Tommy No.
Martha Is it the way I can cook, then?
Tommy No.
Martha Well is it because I'm witty, charming, talented and unassuming, then?
Tommy No. It's none of those.
Martha (*defeated*) Oh, I give in.
Tommy That's right.

SONG 13

After the song they exit R

Pye and Peas enter L

Peas (*loudly*) Come on. Everybody out. (*He looks around*) Here—they've escaped. Hopped it.
Pye Oh, blimey. Quick. We've got to tell the Baron. Come on.

They dash out

Black-out

SCENE 7

The City Square. Daylight

As the Lights come up the Square is empty

Colin, Jack, Jill, the Duke and Mother Shipton hurry in R. *The men are armed*

Colin (*glancing around*) We're in luck. Not a sign of anybody, as yet.
Jack Good. That'll give us a chance to work out exactly what we're going to do.
Duke You mean—you've thought of something?
Jill Yes. Jack and I are going to hide, but the rest of you must stay here so that the Baron can't miss seeing you when the fun starts.
Duke But—but—er—can't I hide as well? I mean—I'm sure I've had a lot more practice than you have.
Colin No, no, Your Grace. We need you with us. There's bound to be a big crowd here when the Baron arrives, and we've got to mingle with it. The moment he begins to speak, we make as much disturbance as we can, and while he's trying to see what's causing it . . .
Jack *We* rush out of hiding, snatch the Talisman from him . . .
Jill And rescue Melody.
Colin Once that's out of his hands, I'll teach him a lesson he'll never forget.
Duke But what if something goes wrong? If we don't get the Talisman?

Colin Then we've lost everything. (*Brightly*) But I don't think it's going to come to that, is it, Mother Shipton?

Tommy and Martha hurry in R

Tommy (*to the audience; breathlessly*) Hiya, kids.
Martha Quick. We've just spotted old Snatcher coming up Ousegate. Fetch me a big spade, somebody.
Duke Surely you're not going to hit him with *that*?
Martha Of course not. I'm going to dig a great big hole in the middle of the Square, and with a bit of luck he'll fall straight down it and knock himself silly.
Tommy Oh, don't be ridiculous, Martha. You can't do that. He'd know it was a trap the minute he saw all that soil piled up.
Martha No he wouldn't. Because I'll dig *another* hole and *bury* it.
Colin (*glancing off* UL) Look out. He's heading this way. (*To Jack and Jill*) Hide.

Jack and Jill dash off as the Citizens of York begin to enter the Square

Voice (*off*) Make way for His Grace, the *new* Grand Duke of York.

Before the Baron has time to enter, several of the Citizens recognize Frederick and greet him with delight. Colin and the others quickly motion them to conceal the Duke and this they do. Colin, Martha, Tommy, Jack and Jill mingle with the Crowd

Baron Snatcher enters UL, *followed by Melody and two Guards. The Baron marches* DC, *sneering*

Baron My loyal subjects . . .
Crowd Boo! Hiss! Etc.
Baron Quiet, you miserable dogs. (*He raises the Talisman*)

The Crowd falls silent

As your new Grand Duke and future ruler of the Universe, I have a very important announcement to make. This very day, the beautiful Miss Melody and I—(*he pulls her to his side*)—are to be married in the Minster . . . (*He leers*)

The Crowd gasps

Colin (*from hiding*) Over my dead body, you ugly old twister.
Baron (*startled*) Who said that?
Martha (*hidden*) *I* did.
Baron (*turning*) What?
Tommy (*hidden*) And so did *I*.

The Baron looks around in confusion

Baron I command you to show yourself.
Colin With the greatest of pleasure. (*He steps out of hiding*)
Baron The Gypsy boy.

Martha, Tommy, Duke and Mother Shipton also come out of hiding

And the others.

He holds the Talisman aloft to cast a spell, but before he can speak, Jack and Jill dash out of hiding and snatch it from his hands, pulling Melody away also

Ahhhhhhhhhhh! The Talisman.

Jack Your Grace. (*He tosses it to Frederick*) Quickly.

Duke (*flustered*) Ooo-er. (*He fumbles with it*)

Baron Guards. (*He signals to them*)

The Guards rush at Frederick

Melody Uncle Frederick. Look out.

Duke (*lifting the Talisman*) I wish this Talisman had never been found.

There is a crash of thunder and Black-out. When the Lights come up again, the Talisman is gone

Colin And now let's see how tough you are without magic to help you. (*He draws his sword*)

Baron (*smirking*) That's something you'll never find out, Gypsy boy. You see . . . I still have *this*. (*He produces the Sword of Chivalry*)

Jack (*recognizing it*) Colin. It's the enchanted sword you killed the Guardian with.

The Crowd fall back to make room

Baron How right you are. (*He laughs*)

The Baron lunges at Colin who evades the thrust. With shouted encouragement from the Crowd, Colin battles with the Baron, but the magic sword is too powerful to resist. Colin's sword is knocked out of his hand and all gasp as the Baron raises his sword for the final blow

Prepare to die.

Mother Shipton quickly steps forward

Mother Shipton One moment. Ere you strike that blow, here's news to
think upon.
No Gypsy boy before you stands, but Grand Duke
Frederick's long-lost son.

Everyone reacts with astonishment

When twenty years ago his cradle fell from yonder
tree—(*she indicates*)—
A passing Gypsy caught the child and brought him
safe to me.
Because I saw what lay ahead, the things that had to
be,
I charged the man to raise the boy and make him
strong as he.

> That task he did. The lad grew strong as he became a
> man.
> I thought if he were sharp and bold he'd put a stop to
> *your* vile plan.
> But now upon the City Square, it seems that fate
> intended
> Right from the start he'd *lose* the fight. My vision now
> has ended.
> (*She turns her back as if in sorrow and her head droops*)

Baron (*leering at Colin*) So—that old fool is your father, is he? All the
more reason for polishing you off. (*He lifts his sword*)

Duke (*loudly*) No. You shan't kill him. You shan't.

*The Duke draws his sword and rushes at the Baron. A second fight begins
which may be as slapstick as possible, but such is the ferocity of the Duke's
attack, the Baron is defeated*

Baron (*dropping the magic sword and falling to his knees*) Mercy, mercy.

*The Crowd all cheer. Jack snatches up the magic sword, and the Guards are
seized by the Crowd. Martha and Tommy grab the Baron. Melody rushes to
the Duke and hugs him tightly*

Melody Uncle Frederick. You were *wonderful.*

Duke (*modestly*) Pshaw. It was nothing. Nothing at all.

Mother Shipton (*sparkling*) Well done, Grand Duke. I knew
> To save your new-found son you'd fight.
> Now greet him like a father should . . .
> Embrace him. Hold him tight.

Duke (*overwhelmed*) My little boy. (*He rushes to him*)

Colin (*embracing him*) Father.

Martha (*tearfully*) Oooh, doesn't it break your heart?

Baron (*wailing*) I can't understand it. How on earth could that little pip-
squeak beat my magic sword with *his* bit of rusty old tin?

There is a crash of thunder and Maleficent enters L in a green light

Everyone reacts

Maleficent The answer's simple, Baron S. 'Twas I who put you in a
mess.
> The moment Frederick destroyed that Talisman, its spells
> were void,
> And in that self-same thunder crack, my magic pow'rs came
> rushing back.
> It only took a teeny spell to fix your sword, and thus you
> fell;
> Which proves once more it's time ill-spent, to try and best
> Maleficent.

Baron (*grovelling to her*) But it was a joke. A prank. I swear it. I was
going to give you your powers back in a little while.

Maleficent Silence! (*She glances around*) To this tender scene
                I'll make *my* contribution.
                Prepare yourselves for what's to come . . .
                It's time for retribution. (*She raises her wand*)

*The Baron yells and covers his eyes. Others wait for the blow to fall.
Maleficent suddenly smiles*

            Ooooooh! If only you could see your faces. (*She laughs merrily*)

Everyone looks bewildered

Tommy Here. She's having hysterics.
Martha Quick. Slap her across the face with the flat of a steam shovel.
Colin (*cautiously*) Is something wrong?
Maleficent (*shaking her head*) Not a thing, my gallant young poppinjay.
    Quite the opposite, in fact. (*She laughs again*)
Melody Aren't you—angry with us any more?
Maleficent Not in the least. You see—I've realized at last what a very
    unpleasant fairy I must have been. It's no wonder nobody liked me.
    For *centuries* hardly anyone has *spoken* to me. I didn't realize it was
    because of my bad temper, and the more people ignored me, the more
    bad-tempered and spiteful I became.
Martha Well I can't say we hadn't noticed.
Maleficent It wasn't till I lost my magic powers that I found out I didn't
    have a friend in the world. Even the other fairies didn't want to know
    me. You can imagine how surprised I was when the Grand Old Duke
    tried to help me—especially after all I'd done to him—but when the
    one person I *had* helped turned his back on me, I made a vow that if
    ever I *did* get my powers back, I'd turn over a new leaf and become the
    nicest fairy that ever lived.
Duke (*stunned*) I can't believe it.
Maleficent Thanks to all of you, I got them back sooner than I expected,
    so I hurried here to help you defeat *that* double crossing old twister—
    (*she indicates the Baron*)—and make up for all the nasty things I've done.
Colin Does that mean you'll bring the Grand Duke's army back to life?
Maleficent (*ruefully*) I'm sorry. That's the one thing I can't do. Only the
    Talisman has that power, and that's gone forever. (*Brightening*) But
    I'll tell you what I *can* do. I'll use the stones to build a great wall around
    the City. That way, your army will protect the City until the end of time.

Everyone looks interested

Duke Well—I suppose that's all right. But what about me? I've got no
    army at all now. In a few years time, everyone will have forgotten me.
Maleficent Not so. To make amends for my great wrongs, a spell I'll
                cast whereby.
                Your name in nursery rhyme and song shall last until the
                seas run dry.
                (*She glares at the Baron*)
                But as for *him*, I do declare it is my firm intention

To wipe his name from human mind. He'll *never* get a
mention.

(*To Mother Shipton*)

You really made me cross at times, and spoiled my little
plans . . .

But now I'm glad you did, my dear. So come. Let's both
shake hands.

They do so

And just to show there's no ill-will remaining in my heart,

A farewell gift I'll make to you to prove you played your
part.

The dropping-well outside your cave shall henceforth have
the power

To turn to stone all objects placed beneath—from shoe to
flower.

There is general reaction

To all the rest I leave the gifts of Wisdom, Health and
Laughter,

Plus one *command*—my dearest wish—live happily ever after.

Maleficent waves her wand and there is a Black-out

The Baron and Maleficent exit

The Lights come up

Jack She's gone. And so's the Baron.
Jill And look. (*She points off*) The new City wall.

Everyone gasps with astonishment

Tommy Never mind about that. What's happened to the Baron's castle
and the hill?

Martha (*amazed*) They've gone. Vanished into thin air.

Mother Shipton (*nodding*)

Quite so. Almost all trace of what transpired upon this day
Has been removed from sight. 'Tis better in a way.

Colin You're right. I don't think any of us will need reminding of all the
adventures we've been through. We'll remember them for the rest of
our lives.

Duke And if we don't, it won't be for want of trying. After all, it's not
every day a father finds his long lost son and sees him marry the loveliest
girl in the City. Come on. Back to my Mansion House and get the
champagne out. We're going to have the biggest party that's ever been
seen in Yorkshire.

Everyone cheers loudly and then sings

SONG 14

All exit laughing merrily after the song

Pye and Peas enter

Pye (*disgustedly*) Huh. Well that's us out of a job again. And we still haven't been paid.

Peas Never mind, old chappie. I think I might have just the thing we're looking for. I got a letter this morning from the Sheriff of Nottingham. (*He produces a letter*) Seems he wants us to look after a couple of youngsters for him. Take them for walks in the woods, etcetera.

Pye Well that sounds simple enough. How soon can we start?

Ad-libbing, they exit arm in arm UL *as—*

the CURTAIN *falls*

SCENE 8

A corridor in the Grand Duke's Mansion House

Song sheet, or as required

SCENE 9

The Mansion House

As the finale music starts the cast walk down as follows:

> Choristers
> Juniors
> Babes
> Pye and Peas
> Mother Shipton and Maleficent
> Jack and Jill
> Baron Snatcher
> Martha and Tommy
> The Grand Old Duke
> Colin and Melody

Melody Our wedding day is dawning.
Colin So pop the champagne cork.
Duke We hope you've all enjoyed the tale of——
All —the Grand Old Duke of York.

CURTAIN

FURNITURE AND PROPERTY LIST

ACT I

SCENE 1

On stage: **Martha Muffett**'s cottage cut out
Houses, shops, etc., cut out
Balloons, puppets, traders' goods, etc. **(Citizens)**

Off stage: Whip **(Baron)**
Broom **(Martha)**
Long envelope containing letter **(Jack)**
Stick with red-cloth bag tied to it **(Colin)**
Small purse **(Melody)**
Knitting **(Soldiers)**

Personal: N.B. the following are used throughout the play
Tommy: watch
Duke: military medals
Maleficent: wand
Mother Shipton: wooden spoon

SCENE 2

On stage: Scattered sticks and twigs

Off stage: Bundle of sticks **(Tommy)**
Bundle of sticks **(Martha)**
Folded paper **(Jill)**
Sword **(Colin)**

SCENE 3

On stage: Suits of armour
Campaign flags
Portraits of the Duke's ancestors

Off stage: Brooms, dusters, etc. **(Servants)**
Folded paper **(Colin)**
Sword **(Colin)**

SCENE 4

On stage: Nil

SCENE 5

On stage: **Martha Muffett**'s cottage cut out
Houses, shops, etc., cut out

Off stage: Lantern **(Watchman)**
Sword **(Colin)**
Sword **(Jack)**
Saucepan **(Jill)**
Weapon **(Martha)**
Weapon **(Tommy)**
Several large boxes **(Baron, Pye** and **Peas)**

ACT II

SCENE 1

On stage: Campfire. *Over it:* cauldron
Pile of shoes
Various wares for **Gypsies**

Off stage: Swords **(Guards)**
Pound note **(Pye)**
Ten pound notes **(Peas)**

SCENE 2

On stage: Nil

Off stage: Lanterns resembling flower heads **(Babes)**
Long velvet cushion. *On it:* gleaming sword **(Two Pixies)**

SCENE 3

On stage: Large rock. *Behind it:* casket containing Talisman
Small rock

Off stage: Sword **(Colin)**
Giant spider **(Stage-management)**
Picnic basket. *In it:* sandwiches, mallet **(Martha)**
Swords **(Guards)**
Sword **(Pye)**
Sword **(Peas)**
Sword **(Baron)**

SCENE 4

On stage: Nil

Off stage: Swords **(Guards)**

SCENE 5

On stage: Huge throne

Off stage: Swords **(Guards)**

Personal: **Baron:** Talisman

SCENE 6

On stage: Nil

Off stage: Swords **(Guards)**
Rusty sword **(Duke)**

SCENE 7

On stage: **Martha Muffett**'s cottage cut out
Houses, shops, etc., cut out

Off stage: Sword **(Colin)**
Sword **(Jack)**
Rusty sword **(Duke)**
Gleaming sword **(Baron)**
Letter **(Peas)**

Personal: **Baron:** Talisman

SCENE 8

On stage: Song sheet or as required

SCENE 9

On stage: Full set as required

LIGHTING PLOT

Property fittings required: campfire effect
Several simple internal and external settings

ACT I

To open: Full exterior daylight, bright and sunny

Cue 1	**Maleficent** enters *Green spot on* **Maleficent**	(Page 13)
Cue 2	**Maleficent** exits *Fade green spot*	(Page 13)
Cue 3	**Mother Shipton:** ". . . and sing—or grieve." *Black-out*	(Page 14)
Cue 4	As SCENE 2 opens *Effect of woodland glade lighting, sunset*	(Page 14)
Cue 5	**Maleficent** enters *Green spot on* **Maleficent**	(Page 17)
Cue 6	**Maleficent** exits with the Baron *Fade green spot*	(Page 19)
Cue 7	**Mother Shipton** waves the spoon *Black-out*	(Page 19)
Cue 8	As SCENE 3 opens *Full interior lighting for Mansion House*	(Page 19)
Cue 9	**Maleficent** enters *Green spot on* **Maleficent**	(Page 25)
Cue 10	**Maleficent** exits *Fade green spot*	(Page 26)
Cue 11	**Melody** and **Colin** begin to move away *Lights start to fade*	(Page 26)
Cue 12	**Colin** and **Melody** exit *Fade quickly to Black-out*	(Page 26)
Cue 13	As SCENE 4 opens *Bring up front stage lighting to full*	(Page 26)
Cue 14	At the end of the dance routine *Black-out*	(Page 26)
Cue 15	As SCENE 5 opens *Effect of early morning half-light on City Square*	(Page 27)
Cue 16	**Maleficent** enters *Green spot on* **Maleficent**	(Page 27)
Cue 17	**Maleficent** exits *Fade green spot*	(Page 28)

Cue 18	As the **Duke** sings	(Page 29)
	Gradually bring up lighting to full	
Cue 19	**Maleficent** enters	(Page 32)
	Green spot on **Maleficent**	
Cue 20	**Maleficent** flourishes her wand	(Page 32)
	Lights flicker	

ACT II

To open: Effect of exterior moonlight and glow from campfire

Cue 21	**Maleficent** enters	(Page 39)
	Green spot on **Maleficent**	
Cue 22	**Maleficent** exits	(Page 40)
	Fade green spot	
Cue 23	**Baron, Pye** and **Peas** start to exit	(Page 41)
	Black-out	
Cue 24	As Scene 2 opens	(Page 41)
	Effect of evening light on Rocky Gorge	
Cue 25	Two **Pixies** wave good-bye	(Page 42)
	Fade to Black-out	
Cue 26	As Scene 3 opens	(Page 42)
	Subdued overall lighting in cavern with red, green and blue effect visible from within tunnel	
Cue 27	The **Guardian** appears	(Page 47)
	Flash of lightning	
Cue 28	As **Mother Shipton** holds up the Talisman	(Page 48)
	White spot on **Maleficent**	
Cue 29	**Maleficent** exits	(Page 48)
	Fade white spot	
Cue 30	**Baron Snatcher** holds up the casket	(Page 49)
	Fade to Black-out	
Cue 31	As Scene 4 opens	(Page 50)
	Evening light effect on Hillside	
Cue 32	The **Duke** exits	(Page 52)
	Black-out	
Cue 33	As Scene 5 opens	(Page 52)
	Full general lighting in the Throneroom	
Cue 34	**Pye** and **Peas** exit	(Page 56)
	Black-out	
Cue 35	As Scene 6 opens	(Page 57)
	Subdued light effect on backcloth	
Cue 36	**Pye** and **Peas** exit	(Page 59)
	Black-out	
Cue 37	As Scene 7 opens	(Page 59)
	Effect of bright daylight on the City Square	
Cue 38	**Duke:** "... never been found."	(Page 61)
	Black-out then after a pause the Lights come up as before	

Cue 39	**Maleficent** enters	(Page 62)
	Green spot on **Maleficent**	
Cue 40	**Maleficent** waves her wand	(Page 64)
	Black-out. After a pause bring up the Lights as before but without green spot	
Cue 41	As SCENE 8 opens	(Page 65)
	Spot on Song Sheet or as required	
Cue 42	As SCENE 9 opens	(Page 65)
	Bring up lighting to full for Finale	

EFFECTS PLOT

ACT I

Cue 1	At the end of Song 4 *Flourish of trumpets*	(Page 11)
Cue 2	**Baron:** ". . . half the City to do it." *Loud crash of thunder*	(Page 13)
Cue 3	**Duke:** ". . . thought she was dead." *Crash of thunder*	(Page 25)
Cue 4	**Maleficent:** ". . . Goodnight." *Crash of thunder*	(Page 26)
Cue 5	**Pye:** ". . . scared her off." *Crash of thunder*	(Page 27)
Cue 6	**Colin:** ". . . can you?" *Crash of thunder*	(Page 32)
Cue 7	**Maleficent** flourishes her wand *Great crash*	(Page 32)

ACT II

Cue 8	**Duke:** ". . . I'll—I'll . . ." *Crash of thunder*	(Page 39)
Cue 9	**Duke:** ". . . never been found." *Crash of thunder*	(Page 61)
Cue 10	**Baron:** ". . . rusty old tin?" *Crash of thunder*	(Page 62)

MADE AND PRINTED IN GREAT BRITAIN BY
LATIMER TREND & COMPANY LTD PLYMOUTH

MADE IN ENGLAND